Sacred Fire

Practicing Devotion to the Heart of Jesus

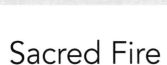

Sacred Fire

Practicing Devotion to the Heart of Jesus

Philip Michael Bulman

Laudate Press
Montgomery Village, Maryland

ISBN: 0990325806
ISBN 13: 978-0-9903258-0-2

Front cover image: Stained glass, Lanckorona, Poland
Back cover image: Stained glass, St. Michael the Archangel
Church, Findlay, Ohio, Creative Commons License
Cover design by Vanessa Maynard

To Ben and Charlie, my amazing sons

May the sacred fire consume our hearts unhindered and make of them thrones worthy of a holy love.

Saint Margaret Mary

Table of Contents

ix

Acknowledgments

I am deeply indebted to all the people who have contributed to the development and understanding of the Sacred Heart devotion over the centuries, many of whom are unknown to us.

Thanks to the publishers who granted permission to reprint excerpts from previously published works.

A special thanks to Doug Sharafinski, who once brought much of my manuscript back from the brink of digital oblivion. I want to extend heartfelt thanks to Mary Ferguson for her many suggestions and prayers.

Over the years I learned a great deal about scripture by listening to the homilies of Father Francis Martin of the Archdiocese of Washington, DC. Some of the ideas expressed in this book are his; any misinterpretations of scripture are mine.

My brothers and sisters at the Mother of God Community in Gaithersburg, Maryland, and the Secular Carmelite Community of the Sacred Heart in Frederick, Maryland, have given me years of fellowship and prayer, and I thank all of you.

I would like to thank the Blessed Virgin Mary, Saint Faustina, Saint Francis de Sales and Saint Teresa of the Andes for reasons known to each of them.

Most of all, I want to thank the Lord Jesus Christ for all His blessings—past, present and future. My prayer is that everyone who reads this book will come to taste of the ineffable sweetness to be found in the infinite depths of His Sacred Heart.

Introduction

Years ago I felt inspired to learn more about the Sacred Heart devotion. At the time I was living in a parish named in honor of Saint Margaret Mary, and I have always suspected that she had something to do with my sudden, intense interest. This has been a fascinating journey that has yielded many discoveries. Notably, the devotion has had a tremendous influence on many members of the Carmelite order, a development that has gone largely unnoticed. More important, my own relationship with God has changed over time. I have felt more gratitude for the sacraments, more hopeful and trusting.

Devotion to the Sacred Heart of Jesus may be the simplest way for Roman Catholics to enter into an intimate relationship with God. With its emphasis on the presence of Jesus in the Eucharist and on God's revelations in scripture, the devotion helps us to bring some of the graces available at Mass into our daily lives. Millions have practiced the devotion over the centuries; many of them are now our heavenly intercessors.

The first part of this book introduces the devotion and follows the series of stunning revelations Jesus made to some of His chosen servants in recent centuries. The second section covers various aspects of the devotion; these chapters may be read in any order. Long book introductions are usually boring, so I simply urge the reader to approach this text prayerfully. If you respond to the Heart of Jesus by opening your own heart, He will pour out His blessings upon you.

Part 1

A Heart Open to All of Humanity

One

The Pierced Heart

And I will pour out on the house of David and the inhabitants of Jerusalem a spirit of compassion and supplication, so that, when they look on him whom they have pierced, they shall mourn for him, as one mourns for an only child, and weep bitterly over him, as one weeps over a firstborn.

Zechariah 12:10

Come to me, all who labor and are heavy laden, and I will give you rest. Take my yoke upon you, and learn from me; for I am gentle and lowly in heart, and you will find rest for your souls. For my yoke is easy, and my burden is light.

Matthew 11:28–30

> But one of the soldiers pierced his
> side with a spear, and at once there
> came out blood and water. He who
> saw it has borne witness—his testi-
> mony is true, and he knows that he
> tells the truth—that you also may
> believe.
>
> John 19:34–35

In the beginning Jesus revealed His Heart at the moment of creation.

All things were created through the Father's Word, the Word Who would become flesh to bring the luminous splendor of divine life to humanity. At creation the Word, eternally determined to become man at the Father's behest, gave the first intimations of what His human and divine Heart are like.

God is love. Creation, which would generate countless creatures, was an act of love that called light and life out of the dark void of nothingness. God is changeless, and creation imparted an atomic structure to the physical world that is stable in its essence. God is playful, and the Eternal Word rejoiced in creation and delighted in sprinkling the heavens and the earth with beauty, both hidden and apparent.

God, in the ineffable embrace of the Holy Trinity, is intimacy, unfathomable tenderness and the infinite joy that inevitably springs from communion. Jesus, through His Sacred Heart,

4

invites us to share that embrace, joy and endless communion.

The Bible uses the word *heart* in several ways. While *heart* may denote a physical organ, much more often it describes the innermost core or essence of God, a person or a situation. Jesus spoke explicitly of His Heart on several occasions, but He revealed His innermost being routinely during His public ministry as He taught, fasted, prayed, healed, laughed, wept, loved and raised the dead to new life. Then He revealed His Heart anew as He suffered, bled and died. Still, that wasn't enough. After death, Jesus willed that His side be opened in a visible sign that the treasures of His Heart would cleanse, heal and sanctify wounded humanity. His Heart is now forever open.

John's Gospel is unique in describing how a soldier pierced the side of Christ. And the fourth Gospel is unique in other ways as well. Here we have the revelation of the Father. Jesus repeatedly taught about the Father and His exquisite care for us. In John we also have the promise of the Holy Spirit, Who would give us true wisdom and understanding. And perhaps most significantly for lovers of the Sacred Heart, we have repeated references to someone who is characterized as the "beloved disciple" or "the disciple whom Jesus loved."

The first mention of the beloved disciple occurs on "the evening of love," as Saint Therese of Lisieux would later call it, when Jesus celebrated

Passover with His followers. On the night before Jesus died, the night of the first Eucharist, we find the beloved disciple lying close to the breast of Jesus. The next mention of the disciple whom Jesus loved is at the Crucifixion. Jesus gave His mother to the beloved disciple, who took her into his home from that day on. The beloved disciple emerged again on the day of Resurrection, accompanying Peter to the empty tomb. Then, in a mysterious event after the Resurrection, Jesus appeared on a shore as the disciples were fishing. At first they didn't know Him. The beloved disciple was the first to recognize Him; he said, "It is the Lord!"

Who is the beloved disciple? Why does the beloved one remain unnamed?

Some early biblical commentators speculated that John declined to name himself out of humility. But others have inferred that John deliberately left the beloved disciple unnamed to help us understand that each of us is called to become the beloved disciple. Jesus invites us to rest close to His breast, to listen to the rapturous rhythms of His Sacred Heart, to receive Him in the Eucharist, to love His holy mother and take her into our homes. He invites us to gaze on His pierced Heart and contemplate His love. Jesus welcomes us into His Heart so we may know the glorious truth of the Resurrection. He invites us to come to know Him so intimately in the depths of our own hearts that we will be able to recognize

Him even in times of darkness, even when others fail to recognize Him, and proclaim with absolute delight and certainty that He is the Lord.

Origen, an early Christian who wrote extensively about the Bible, gave a striking commentary about the Gospels. "The Gospels are the firstfruits of the Scriptures. But the firstfruits of the Gospels is the Gospel according to John whose meaning no one can understand who has not leaned on Jesus' breast or received Mary from Jesus to be his mother also."

Here we find a secret of the Sacred Heart devotion. Through this devotion we enter an intimate, dynamic relationship with Jesus. We do not simply read the Gospel or hear it read anymore; we start to experience the Gospel, understand it and live it. Ultimately, Jesus transforms us as we learn to live the Gospel. Each disciple of the Sacred Heart gradually and mystically becomes the beloved disciple. The Sacred Heart of Jesus is open to all and offers a joyful path of discipleship that leads to everlasting life.

While John may have been the first disciple to regard himself as being devoted to the Heart of Jesus, various early Christians and succeeding generations adopted practices centered on the Scriptures and the Eucharist that became precursors to the modern devotion. Christians studied the Bible and discovered in the Scriptures the foundations of the Sacred Heart devotion in various ways, as we shall see. And Christians viewed the Blood and Water that flowed from the pierced side of Jesus as a great source of blessing, giving birth to the sacramental life of the Church. Holy Mass, incorporating the essential elements of Scripture and the Eucharist, became the preferred form of community worship. For more than a thousand years, Christians drew on these sources, and Christian writers mentioned the Heart of Jesus repeatedly. Then Jesus Himself began to shape the devotion to His Heart in new ways.

Timothy T. O'Donnell, a great scholar of the Sacred Heart devotion, states that the first recorded apparition in which Jesus revealed His Heart as a sign of His love for humanity involved Saint Lutgarde (1182–1246), who would become a Benedictine sister and later join the Cistercian order. Jesus revealed Himself to her and offered her an exchange of hearts.

During this era Jesus started to reveal His Heart to laypeople and vowed religious alike. One example is Blessed Angela of Foligno (1248–1309), a wife and mother who lived, by her own account, in a state of serious sin for many years. She eventually had a deep conversion experience, and God granted her many mystical favors. Angela recounted an experience of seeing Christ on the cross. "He then called me to place my mouth to the wound in his side. It seemed to me that I saw and drank the blood, which was freshly flowing from his side. His intention was to make me understand that by this blood he would cleanse me."

Jesus also revealed Himself to Saint Gertrude the Great during this time. Saint Gertrude's writings had a profound influence on the Sacred Heart devotion, an influence that continues to this day.

Saint Catherine of Sienna (1347–1380), a lay Dominican who is a Doctor of the Church, had great devotion to the Heart of Jesus, which her famous work, *The Dialogue*, often mentions. In one passage she recounted how she asked Jesus about His Heart.

"'Why, gentle spotless Lamb, since you were dead when your side was opened, did you want your heart to be pierced and parted?' He answered: 'There were plenty of reasons, but I shall tell you one of the chief. My longing for humankind was infinite, but the actual deed of bearing pain and torment was finite and could never show all the love I had. This is why I wanted you to see my inmost heart, so that you would see that I loved you more than finite suffering could show.'"

Many other Christians, including some great saints, mentioned the Heart of Christ in their writings. Countless others, both famous and unknown, came to know His Heart through prayer and meditation, the Scriptures and the Eucharist. Then a significant shift took place because of the efforts of Saint John Eudes (1601–1670). He was a great promoter of devotion to the Hearts of Jesus and Mary and composed Mass texts that could be used to honor the Sacred Heart. He founded the Congregation of Jesus and Mary and even received permission to have his congregation observe a Feast of the Sacred Heart. His pioneering efforts laid a solid, liturgical groundwork for the Sacred Heart devotion.

Yet it was not until the late seventeenth century that devotion to the Sacred Heart would take on a particular form because of the Lord's revelations to Saint Margaret Mary. Besides showing Himself to her many times, Jesus made specific requests about how the Church should practice devotion to His Heart. Among other things, He asked for the establishment of a special feast day in honor of His Heart, called for Masses honoring His Heart on the first Friday of each month and requested that Christians make a regular Holy Hour in honor of His Passion. As a virtually unknown sister living in a cloistered monastery, Saint Margaret Mary was incapable of carrying out these requests by herself. Saint Claude de la Colombiere, a Jesuit priest, would become her partner in promoting the devotion.

While it would be some years before the Church established the feast day Jesus had requested, devotion to the Sacred Heart spread rapidly following the death of Saint Margaret Mary and the publication of her writings. Laypeople adopted the devotion with great fervor. Images of the Sacred Heart were soon found in homes and churches as Catholics began to experience the great blessings that flowed from the pierced side of Christ. The faithful composed poems and hymns to celebrate their union with the Heart of Jesus. As a result, two significant changes occurred.

Previously, Jesus had sometimes revealed the designs of His Heart through stunning mystical experiences granted to great saints, such as Gertrude and Margaret Mary. With that foundation in place, He now routinely revealed His Heart to sinners, granting them great graces of repentance, conversion and healing.

The other significant change was in how people learned of the Sacred Heart. As the modern devotion spread, many Catholics encountered the Sacred Heart in their families and schools, often as young children. They grew up with the devotion, and it influenced and shaped their spirituality as adults, whether lay or religious. Soon enough, people who had great love for the Sacred Heart entered religious orders, where their devotion served as a catalyst that helped them to reach great heights of sanctity. Several striking examples of this, spread over several hundred years, are found in the Carmelite order.

Meanwhile, some advocates in the Church worked toward the establishment of the Feast of the Sacred Heart Jesus had requested. In 1765 Poland became the first country to receive permission to observe the feast as a nation. The feast was extended to the universal Church in 1856. During the same era, Catholics found their attention drawn to the Sacred Heart in another way.

During an apparition in 1830, Mary appeared to Saint Catherine Laboure in Paris. Mary showed her the design for a medal that could be worn around the neck. On the front is an engraving of Mary, graces streaming from her hands, and the following prayer: "O Mary conceived without sin, pray for us who have recourse to thee." On the reverse the medal includes a large letter *M* mounted by a cross, and beneath that are images of the Hearts of Jesus and Mary. Known today as the Miraculous Medal, it has achieved enormous popularity. Millions of Catholics have worn the medals, keeping these symbols of the Hearts of Jesus and Mary close to their own hearts. In another development that originated in France, Father Francis X. Guatrelet, a Jesuit, founded the Apostleship of Prayer in 1844. This extraordinary organization promotes devotion to the Sacred Heart throughout the world.

In the late nineteenth century, Blessed Mary of the Divine Heart, a Sister of the Good Shepherd order, had a mystical experience in which Jesus asked for the world to be consecrated to His Sacred Heart. Sister Mary's superior sent a letter to the pope with the request in 1898. The pope initially took no action, and a second letter was sent early in 1899.

In April of 1899, Pope Leo XIII approved the great Litany of the Sacred Heart, which remains a popular prayer. The following month he issued *Annum Sacrum,* his encyclical calling for the consecration of the world to the Sacred Heart of Jesus in June of that year. He also urged Catholics throughout the world to pray the litany and make individual acts of consecration to the Sacred Heart during the month of June. Pope Leo described the consecration of the world to the Sacred Heart as the greatest act of his papacy.

The twentieth century saw many events that gave even greater impetus to the Sacred Heart devotion as Jesus responded generously to the global and individual consecrations that had been offered to Him. In 1916 an angel appeared to three children in Fatima, Portugal, to prepare them for the Marian apparitions that would take place the following year. The angel taught them a prayer. "My God, I believe, I adore, I hope and I love you! I ask pardon of You for those who do not believe, do not adore, do not hope and do not love You." Then the angel said to them, "Pray thus. The Hearts of Jesus and Mary are attentive to the voice of your supplications." In 1917 Mary appeared to these children. She asked them to pray the rosary every day and requested that people honor her Immaculate Heart by receiving Communion on the first Saturday of each month. The events at Fatima reaffirmed the importance of devotion to the Hearts of Jesus and Mary.

During the same period, a young Chilean girl who had a deep devotion to the Sacred Heart climbed to great heights of sanctity. Saint Teresa of the Andes would give the world an example of how the Sacred Heart devotion leads people to experience an extraordinary joy born of intimacy with Jesus.

In 1920 Saint Margaret Mary was canonized, sparking a renewed wave of interest in the Sacred Heart devotion. Then in 1925 Pope Pius XI established the Feast of Christ the King and asked the faithful to renew their consecration to the Sacred Heart on that day. Three years later the Pope issued *Miserentissimus Redemptor*, an encyclical focused on acts of reparation to the Heart of Jesus. In 1932 he issued *Caritate Christi Compulsi*, an encyclical calling for prayer and sacrifices directed to the Sacred Heart.

Meanwhile, Jesus was laying the groundwork for a further development of the Sacred Heart devotion that emphasized His mercy. In a series of revelations to Sister Faustina Kowalska of Poland, Jesus called out to sinners in an extraordinary way, inviting them to return to Him and enjoy the infinite blessings of Divine Mercy.

In 1956 Pope Pius XII published *Haurietis Aquas*, his encyclical on the Sacred Heart devotion, in which he urged Christians to study and practice the devotion. "It is altogether impossible to enumerate the heavenly gifts which devotion to the Sacred Heart of Jesus has poured out on the souls of the faithful, purifying them, offering them heavenly strength, rousing them to the attainment of all virtues," he said.

More recent papal documents reveal repeated exhortations to the faithful to adopt the great devotion of love. Pope John Paul II was especially ardent in his promotion of devotion to the Sacred Heart. He offered a series of Angelus meditations, spanning several years, on the Litany of the Sacred Heart, which was one of his favorite prayers. John Paul routinely incorporated references to the Sacred Heart into his homilies and apostolic letters. He made pilgrimages and pastoral visits to several sites associated with the Sacred Heart of Jesus, including Paray-le-Monial, the home of Saint Margaret Mary, and the Divine Mercy Sanctuary in Cracow, Poland. Also, John Paul presided over the canonizations of many saints who had a special devotion to the Sacred Heart, including Saint Claude de la Colombiere, Saint Teresa of the Andes and Saint Faustina. John Paul also decided to have the universal Church observe the Sunday after Easter as Divine Mercy Sunday.

Pope Benedict XVI also promoted the Sacred Heart devotion. He marked the fiftieth anniversary of the publication of *Haurietis Aquas* by writing a letter to the superior general of the Society of Jesus. The Jesuits have been promoters of the devotion for hundreds of years. The following is an excerpt from his letter:

By encouraging devotion to the Heart of Jesus, the Encyclical *Haurietis Aquas* exhorted believers to open themselves to the mystery of God and of his love and to allow themselves to be transformed by it. After 50 years, it is still a fitting task for Christians to continue to deepen their relationship with the Heart of Jesus, in such a way as to revive their faith in the saving love of God and to welcome him ever better into their lives. The Redeemer's pierced side is the source to which the Encyclical *Haurietis Aquas* refers us: we must draw from this source to attain true knowledge of Jesus Christ and a deeper experience of his love. Thus, we will be able to understand better what it means *to know* God's love in Jesus Christ, to experience him, keeping our gaze fixed on him to the point that we *live* entirely on the experience of his love, so that we can subsequently *witness* to it to others.

Indeed, to take up a saying of my venerable Predecessor John Paul II, "In the Heart of Christ, man's heart learns to know the genuine and unique meaning of his life and of his destiny, to understand the value of an authentically Christian life, to keep himself from certain perversions of the human heart, and to unite the filial love for God and the love of neighbor."

Pope Francis has also taught about the Heart of Jesus. In his homily on Divine Mercy Sunday in 2013, he spoke at length about God's mercy, concluding his homily with these words:

> In my own life, I have so often seen God's merciful countenance, his patience; I have also seen so many people find the courage to enter the wounds of Jesus by saying to him: Lord, I am here, accept my poverty, hide my sin in your wounds, wash it away with your blood. And I have always seen that God did just this—he accepted them, consoled them, cleansed them, loved them.
>
> Dear brothers and sisters, let us be enveloped by the mercy of God; let us trust in his patience, which always gives us more time. Let us find the courage to return to his house, to dwell in his loving wounds, allowing ourselves to be loved by him and to encounter his

17

> mercy in the sacraments. We will
> feel his wonderful tenderness, we
> will feel his embrace, and we too
> will become more capable of mercy,
> patience, forgiveness and love.

Jesus uses both public and private revelation to persuade us to gaze on His pierced Heart. His ardent love for us, despite our agonized entrapment in sin, becomes clear as we behold Him on the cross. By coming before the cross with our faults and weaknesses, we hear Him speak tender words of mercy and forgiveness. We receive the gift of His holy mother. We stand with her as we watch Jesus die in an incomparable act of love for the Father and all of humanity. With Mary we witness the thrust of the lance. We, beloved disciples, see the outpouring of blood and water that gives us life.

For centuries Jesus has presented His Heart to sinners, now with this emphasis, now with another emphasis, anticipating our needs. To Saint Margaret Mary, He showed His Heart radiant with flames of love. She understood that the hearts of many people, crippled by sin, had grown cold, and His Heart was the remedy. Saint Teresa of the Andes, still largely unknown outside Latin America, found that her devotion to the Sacred Heart led to an adherence to God's will that produced indescribable joy. In our day, when sadness and depression have become common, her witness to infinite joy provides great hope to beloved disciples who draw close to the Heart of Jesus. And Saint Faustina's message of Divine Mercy touches the hearts of even the most hardened sinners, drawing them back from condemnation and everlasting death as Jesus prepares the world for His return.

We may wonder why Jesus continues to present Himself and His Sacred Heart to us repeatedly in different ways. Perhaps it's because He is—as Saint Teresa of the Andes once described Him—a "Mad Lover." He sees us more clearly than we see ourselves. He knows our secret sins. Jesus knows our hesitations, our weak efforts to change, our failures and relapses. Yet He follows us down all the pathways that lead us away from Him to love us and teach us how to love God, our neighbors and ourselves. He wants us to experience genuine love, for He is love.

He pursues us because He wants our hearts.

In the Sacred Heart devotion, Jesus offers us everything we need to gain everlasting life for ourselves and obtain immeasurable blessings for our loved ones and the entire Mystical Body of Christ. When we gaze on the pierced One on the cross, we first become uncomfortable, even agonized, about our sins. Yet Jesus then helps us to see the infinite treasures of grace that flow from His Heart. Our guilt and fear may make us hesitate to approach Him as we feel ourselves unworthy of these treasures. We may feel exhausted by the pains of life here below, and battered by our countless failures to turn away from sin. In a letter to a friend, Saint Margaret Mary described what we should then do. "As for your entering into His Sacred Heart: enter in! What should you fear, since He invites you to come in and rest there?"

Two

Saint Gertrude
the Great

My beloved has gone down to his
garden,
to the beds of spices,
to pasture his flock in the gardens,
and to gather lilies.
I am my beloved's and my beloved
is mine;
he pastures his flock among the
lilies.

Song of Songs 6:2–3

And I will betroth you to me for
ever; I will betroth you to me in
righteousness and in justice, in
steadfast love, and in mercy. I will
betroth you to me in faithfulness;
and you shall know the Lord.

Hosea 2:19–20

21

> Then he showed me the river of the
> water of life, bright as crystal, flow-
> ing from the throne of God and of
> the Lamb.
> Revelation 22:1

Saint Gertrude the Great of Helfta was born on the Feast of the Epiphany, January 6, 1256, in what is now Germany. Nothing is known about her parents or the first few years of her life; she may have been an orphan. At the age of four, she began living at a monastery of Benedictine nuns in Helfta. She remained there for the rest of her life. Gertrude received a well-rounded education from the sisters that included secular studies, language skills and Latin, which was the universal language of the church. She was a good student and developed a great love of literature. Her life within the Helfta community was unremarkable until she was twenty-five years old. She experienced a vision that changed her and eventually brought about significant changes in the Church for centuries to come.

Gertrude had been troubled and sad for about a month. One day she was in the monastery's dormitory when an elderly religious walked by her. Gertrude bowed to the sister, as was the custom, but when she looked up, she found herself looking at Jesus, who presented Himself to her as a youth. "Soon will come your salvation; why are you so sad? Is it because you have no one to confide in that you are sorrowful?" He asked.

Gertrude found herself suddenly transported in spirit to the monastery's choir room, where Jesus addressed her again. "I will save you. I will deliver you. Do not fear...With my enemies you have licked the dust and sucked honey among thorns. Come back to me now, and I will inebriate you with the torrent of my divine pleasure."

As Jesus spoke, she saw a tall hedge, topped with thorns, separating her from Him. She didn't know how to reach Him and thought she would faint with desire for Him. He reached across to her, lifted her across the hedge and placed her at His side. Saint Gertrude tells of the effect this vision had on her in a passage of her writing she addressed to Jesus. "From that hour, in a new spirit of joyful serenity, I began to follow the way of the sweet odor of your perfumes, and I found your yoke sweet and your burden light which a short time before I had thought to be unbearable."

Here we find Gertrude paraphrasing a passage from scripture where Jesus calls people to discipleship and specifically to a discipleship involving His Sacred Heart. "Come to me, all who labor and are heavy laden, and I will give you rest. Take my yoke upon you, and learn from me; for I am gentle and lowly in heart, and you will find rest for your souls. For my yoke is easy, and my burden is light" (Matt. 11:28–30).

Saint Gertrude's decision to express herself in this way is significant for two reasons: First, it refers to the Heart of Jesus and provides a hint of the experiences she would have in the future. Second, she expressed herself in biblical terms, a method that is characteristic of her writings. Gertrude spent much of her life immersed in scripture studies and had a gift for making difficult passages of the Bible understandable to others. Her synthesis of her loves for the Sacred Heart of Jesus and the Bible contributed to a solid scriptural foundation for the Sacred Heart devotion.

Centuries later, some people charged that the devotion was "new" or not firmly rooted in sacred scripture. Disciples of the Sacred Heart were able to point to the beautiful works of Saint Gertrude to prove the critics wrong on both counts. Two of her books, originally composed in Latin, have been especially influential throughout the centuries. One is the *Legatus Memorialis Abundantiae Divinae Pietatis (Herald of the Memorial of the Abundance of Divine Love)*. The book is available in English under several titles: *The Herald of Divine Love* and *The Life and Revelations of St. Gertrude*. Her other major work, also available in English, is titled *Spiritual Exercises*.

Jesus often presented Himself to Gertrude to reveal the mysteries of His Sacred Heart to her. He told her to write an account of her experiences so future generations would yearn for His Heart. One theme that emerges from His revelations to her is His desire for people to use His Heart to make up for their defects. The Sacred Heart is a gift to Christians that has the power to supply what is wanting in their lives. During some of these mystical experiences, He showed her that His Heart is both human and divine. In addition He led her to understand that suffering can sanctify the soul. On one such occasion, Gertrude was sick in bed, and Jesus came to comfort her. The saint recounts what she experienced.

> He showed me, issuing from his left side as though from the innermost depths of his blessed heart, a stream of flowing water as pure as crystal and as solid. It proceeded to cover his adorable breast like a jewel. I saw that it was transparent, colored in hues of gold and rose, alternating in various ways. With this, the Lord gave me to understand these words: "The sickness from which you are now suffering has so sanctified your soul that whenever for my sake you condescend to others in thought, word, or deed, you will never be far from me, as is shown you in this stream. And just as the gold and rose colors gleam through the purity of the crystal and are enhanced by it, so

> will your intentions be pleasing,
> seen through the cooperation of
> the gold of my divinity and the per-
> fecting power of the patience of the
> rose of my humanity."

This was one of several occasions when Jesus told Saint Gertrude that purity of intention is an important virtue for disciples of the Sacred Heart. When people turn away from prayer and contemplation to undertake other tasks, God doesn't remove Himself from them. Jesus sanctifies the actions of His disciples when they are immersed in prayer or in other works, as long as their intent is to love and serve Him.

On another occasion Saint John the Evangelist appeared to Saint Gertrude on his feast day and led her to the Sacred Heart. This set a precedent, repeated centuries later, when Jesus made the first great revelation about His Sacred Heart to Saint Margaret Mary on December 27, St. John's Feast day. During his appearance to Gertrude, John took her in spirit to heaven. They rested on the bosom of Jesus, with Gertrude on His right side and John on His left side. John explained that he had placed her on the right side of Jesus because she was still in the flesh. "I have therefore placed you at the opening of the Divine Heart, from whence you may drink in all the sweet consolations which flow from it with such impetuous abundance that it is capable of satisfying all who desire to taste thereof," he said.

Saint Gertrude experienced ecstasy as she felt the throbs of the Heart of Jesus. She asked Saint John if he had not had a similar experience at the Last Supper when he rested on the breast of Jesus. He said that he had, and Gertrude asked why he hadn't written more plainly about the Sacred Heart in his Gospel. John explained that such revelations about the Sacred Heart had been reserved "until later ages, that the world might be aroused from its torpor, and animated, when it had grown cold, by hearing of these things."

Gratitude for God's gifts was a hallmark of Saint Gertrude's spirituality. She understood that the Sacred Heart of Jesus is available to anyone who wants to use it as a perfect way to give thanks and praise to the Father. While she stresses devotion to the Heart of Jesus, she knew the devotion led her into a deeper relationship with all three Persons of the Trinity. In addition, she saw Christ's Heart as a universal gift offered to the entire human race. Her response was universal prayer; she often prayed not for herself but in the name of all people—past, present and future. For example, we find this passage in her writings: "With the sweetly melodious harp of your divine heart, through the power of the Holy Spirit, the Paraclete, I sing to you, Lord God, adorable Father, songs of praise and thanksgiving on behalf of all creatures in heaven, on earth, and under the earth; all which are, were, and shall be."

While Saint Gertrude offered such universal prayers, her experiences confirmed that praying to the Sacred Heart of Jesus for individuals was also important. These prayers brought instant, though invisible, results. On one occasion she prayed for a woman who had many defects and imperfections. She immediately saw a river, "pure as crystal," flowing out of the breast of Jesus and into the heart of this person for whom she had prayed so many times. Gertrude asked Jesus why the woman didn't appear to be making any spiritual progress, and He explained that sometimes His graces are like medicines. Most medicines do not result in instantaneous cures, but they gradually and imperceptibly bring the sick person back to health.

Many revelations about the Sacred Heart were closely associated with the Eucharist. One day when Gertrude was about to receive Communion, she had a vision of her soul. Her soul was represented to her as a tree whose roots were planted in the wound of the side of Jesus. As she received Communion, she experienced a great influx of graces, which she perceived as sap flowing to all the branches and fruits of her life. She understood that God is glorified when people receive Communion, drawing graces and life from the Sacred Heart, which enriches them with the virtues of Jesus.

Many of Gertrude's mystical experiences were spousal in nature. She understood that the human soul (regardless of whether a person is male or female) is created to be a bride of Christ. The saint regarded herself as God's lover, and her writings draw heavily from the Song of Songs with its unabashedly erotic imagery. The writings of Saint Bernard undoubtedly influenced her, especially his commentaries on the Song of Songs. For Gertrude receiving the Eucharist was an act of consummation that satisfied the ardent desires of both parties. On one occasion she was giving thanks after receiving Communion, and Jesus spoke to her with these words: "Know that I desired you with my whole heart."

The saint had various mystical experiences that influenced her spirituality. For example, Gertrude received the stigmata in her heart in response to persistent prayers for that favor, as she reported in this passage, which is addressed to Jesus: "I knew in my spirit that I had received the stigmata of your adorable and venerable wounds interiorly in my heart, just as though they had been made on the natural places of the body. By these wounds you not only healed my soul, but you gave me to drink of the inebriating cup of love's nectar." A boundless and expectant faith in God was an integral part of Saint Gertrude's life, which explains how she would seek something like the stigmata and expect to receive it. Jesus once told her to expect such results as a response to prayer in these words: "Confidence alone is sufficient to obtain everything easily."

Another special grace she received was a wound of love in her heart, which appeared to come directly from the Sacred Heart of Jesus. In addition on one Christmas she received the child Jesus into her soul in a sensible way. Saint Gertrude also experienced an exchange of hearts with Jesus on several occasions, as she recalls in this passage addressed to Him: "In addition to all these favors, you have granted me the priceless gift of your familiar friendship, giving me in various ways, to my indescribable delight, the noblest treasure of the divinity, your divine heart, now bestowing it freely, now as a sign of our mutual familiarity, exchanging it with mine."

Gertrude added an important facet to the Sacred Heart devotion because of revelations Jesus presented to her. For centuries Christians had seen the Sacred Heart as a source of blessings for the Church as a whole. Indeed, many people regarded the Church as having been born from the pierced Heart of Christ. However, Gertrude understood that His Heart is a source of graces for individuals as well as for the Church as a body. She also understood that Jesus offers us His Heart so we can actively take advantage of His fathomless generosity. His Heart is a living instrument He invites us to enter and use, not simply a subject for meditation. Saint Gertrude's understanding of this aspect of the Sacred Heart was the result of a revelation from Jesus. One day when she was singing hymns, she was distressed because she thought she was doing such a poor job. Jesus offered her His Heart to make up for all that was lacking in her and spoke to her.

> Behold, here is my heart, the sweetest instrument of the ever adorable Trinity. I hold it in front of the eyes of your heart; it will supply all that you lack, faithfully making up for all that you entrust to it. Because, like a faithful servant who is always ready to do what his lord pleases, from now onward my heart will always cleave to you, so that it may make up at any time for all your negligences…So, without any doubt, my divine heart, recognizing the frailty and inconstancy of human nature, always waits with ineffable longing to supply for whatever you entrust to it, if not by words, at least by a sign, so as to do for you whatever you are unable to do for yourself. Its omnipotence makes it act with ease; its impenetrable wisdom enables it to know what is best; and the goodness which is natural to me makes me desire with sweet and joyous benevolence to accomplish this end.

Here we find a remarkable invitation as Jesus tells us His Heart is always available to us. Just as He took the role of a servant by washing the feet of His disciples, He offers us His Heart as an instrument that makes up for our defects. If we fail to be as attentive or fervent as possible during prayer, we can ask Jesus to make up for our defects through the infinite merits of His Heart.

Jesus repeated this lesson on another occasion. Saint Gertrude found that she had passed almost an entire day one Friday without thinking about the Crucifixion. As evening fell she offered a prayer to Jesus, lamenting that she hadn't thought about His suffering sometime during the day. Jesus told her that His Sacred Heart would make up for her negligences in response to her prayer.

"That which you were neglecting, I myself have supplied for you. For instance, every hour I gathered into my heart what you should have been recollecting in your own heart, and afterward my heart was exceedingly full. Almost bursting with great desire, I have longed for this hour when you would make this intention your own. Now, with that intention of yours, I want to offer to God my Father all that which I have supplied for you throughout this day, for without your intention my action could not be so conducive to your salvation."

Jesus also appeared to Saint Gertrude during Mass one day and explained that the gift of

free will enables everyone to draw from the treasures of His Sacred Heart. He used the imagery
of a golden tube to reveal this lesson to her. "I
have given to everyone a golden tube of such
power that he may draw whatever he desires
from the infinite depths of my divine heart," He
said. During this vision she saw the members of
her community gathered around Jesus, using
their golden tubes (that is, their freedom) to
draw graces and blessings from Him. Some drew
graces directly from His Sacred Heart and experienced a great torrent of blessings. Others drew
graces from His hands. Saint Gertrude saw that
those who had conformed themselves to God's
will were the ones who drank directly from the
Sacred Heart. The others depended more on their
own wills and their own efforts instead of abandoning themselves to divine Providence. The first
group received spiritual and temporal blessings
in great abundance; the second group, while still
receiving precious graces, had more difficulty in
getting temporal and spiritual blessings.

While the will is a great gift from God, the most
ardent disciples of the Sacred Heart learn to surrender their wills to Him. Saint Gertrude once had
a serious fever that left her sick and soaked with
sweat. As she wondered whether the fever would
diminish or perhaps grow worse, Jesus appeared
to her. He stretched out His hands, and she saw
that He offered her health with one hand and illness with the other. She brushed past His hands

to reach His Heart, where she reclined, asking Him to decide whether she should receive continued sickness or health. He then told her that because she was turning her will over to Him, "I am sending all the sweetness and delight of my divine heart into you."

A significant facet of Saint Gertrude's devotion to the Sacred Heart was her emphasis on the Passion. To Gertrude devotion to the Sacred Heart and the Passion were intimately intertwined because Jesus would sometimes present these ideas to her simultaneously. He once told her that when people look at a crucifix, the experience should be a source of inspiration. They should understand that He would be willing to suffer all the pains He'd endured during His earthly life to save any one person. "See how I hung upon the cross for love of you, naked and despised, my body covered with wounds and every limb pulled out of joint. And now my heart is moved with such sweet charity toward you that, if it were expedient for your salvation, and if you could be saved in no other way, I would bear for you alone all that you may imagine I bore for the whole world," He said.

Saint Gertrude's emphasis on the Passion came in part from an experience she had while meditating on the sufferings of Jesus. God taught her that meditating on the Passion was more fruitful than meditating on any other part of Christ's life. Reading the scriptural accounts of the Passion prepares people to receive the great fruits of the Passion. However, Gertrude's spirituality involved going beyond meditating on the Passion to imitating it, because she saw such imitation as the perfect way to follow Jesus. Her writings stress the virtues that Jesus showed throughout His life, and especially during His Passion: patience in adversity, a refusal to take revenge, obedience to the Father's will and a passionate, prayerful love of one's enemies.

While the Heart of Jesus stopped beating and was pierced for love of us on Calvary, Saint Gertrude knew that His Heart is alive, filling heaven and earth with blessings. She once had to miss a sermon at her monastery because she was sick. When she told Jesus how grieved she was about missing the sermon, He told her that He would preach to her Himself. He placed her against His Heart, allowing her to hear two distinct pulsations from this unsurpassed source of blessings, then explained what she was hearing.

> Each of these two pulsations brings about man's salvation in three ways. The first pulsation effects the salvation of sinners; the second, that of the just. With the first pulsation, first, I address God the Father, ceaselessly appeasing him and leading him to have mercy upon sinners. Second, I invoke all

my saints, excusing the sinner with fraternal fidelity, and urging them to pray for him. Third, I address the sinner himself, calling upon him to repent, and awaiting his conversion with ineffable longing.

With the second pulsation, first, I address God the Father, inviting him to rejoice with me for having shed my precious blood to such good purpose for the redemption of the just, in whose hearts I now find so many delights. Second, I address all the heavenly hosts, inviting them to praise the lives of the just, and to thank me for the benefits I have already bestowed on them, and for those I will bestow in the future. Third, I address the just themselves, lavishing various favors on them for their salvation and admonishing them to progress from day to day and from hour to hour. And just as the pulsations of the human heart are not impeded by seeing or hearing or by any manual work, but always maintain their regular motion, so the government and disposition of heaven and earth and the whole universe can never affect in the very least these twofold

> pulsations of my divine heart, still
> them, modify them, or in any way
> hinder them, until the end of time.

Here Jesus reveals His Heart as a lavish fountain of salvation for sinners and saints alike. His Heart pours forth a constant shower of graces, and each of us can drink freely of the life-giving waters that spring in torrents from this heavenly source. Indeed, Jesus longs to bless us so much that His charity moves Him to reward us for holy desires alone.

Once when Saint Gertrude's community was asked to set up a new monastery in a different location, the saint found she was full of enthusiasm for the project. However, she had become so sick that she believed she was close to death. Her enthusiasm was so unrealistic that she realized she probably didn't have the strength to make the trip to the new location. Then she prayed to God, asking Him why He'd allowed so many different desires to fill her mind when they would never come to fruition. He explained that this was yet another of His ways to bless His disciples.

> Friends often enjoy talking
> together about many things which
> will never come to pass. And some-
> times, too, a friend will propose to
> another some difficult project, so
> that he may have a certain proof of

his friend's fidelity and, more particularly, of the generosity of his good will toward himself. I, too, delight in proposing to my chosen ones many difficult projects which will never come about, in order to have proof of their love for me and their fidelity, so that I may reward them afterward for these great things which they will in fact never have the opportunity of doing, because I look upon their good will alone as though it were the accomplishment of their good intentions.

Jesus also recommended His Heart to her as a balm against the inevitable disappointments that arise in friendships. Once when Saint Gertrude experienced some distress and disappointment in a friend, Jesus told her that He sometimes allows such incidents to draw someone close to Him. "I permit your friends sometimes to cause you pain so that, never finding perfect fidelity in any creature, you will come running back the more eagerly to me, knowing that with me alone you will find an unchanging abundance of joy and fidelity." Jesus then lifted her onto his breast to console her. Then He offered her His Heart, saying, "Look, my beloved, at the very core of my heart, and consider carefully with what fidelity I have disposed and managed everything you have ever asked me to do for you, in the way that is most profitable for the perfection and salvation of your soul. And now consider whether you can reproach me for the least infidelity to you." He then transformed her pain into a vision of golden flowers.

Saint Gertrude had many different ways of thinking about and experiencing the Sacred Heart. For example, she saw the Heart of Jesus as an ideal home in this life, a place where we could be sheltered from evil influences, as this passage from her *Spiritual Exercises* illustrates: "Ah! ah! Bright Jesus, through the love by which God was made human you came to seek and to save what was lost. Enter now into me, O my cherished one, and in turn lead me into you. Hide me in the firmest rock of your fatherly defense. In the cavern of your most gracious heart hide me away from all that is not you, O dearest of all dear ones."

Indeed, Gertrude regarded life in the Sacred Heart as a way to prepare for death, because those who live in the Heart of God are purified and become worthy to enter heaven. Another passage from her *Spiritual Exercises* illustrates this point. "Pray the Lord to lead you into the pleasure garden of his divine heart that you may bathe there seven times in the Jordan of the merits of his life and passion and that, on the day you depart this life, purged from every spot, all beautiful, you may be led into the inner chamber of his divine love."

Remarkably, Saint Gertrude's experiences at the Helfta monastery were not unique. She was one of three holy women associated with Helfta who received revelations from Jesus about His Sacred Heart. The other two were Saint Mechthild of Hackeborn and Mechthild of Magdeburg. While Gertrude was well known in her lifetime and often sought after as a spiritual adviser, the books of her contemporaries at Helfta were more influential than her books for several centuries following her death.

Gertrude's works, however, enjoyed a revival beginning in the sixteenth century and remain popular to this day. Her books influenced many people, including Saint Francis de Sales and Saint Philip Neri. Saint John Eudes, who was renowned for his tender devotion to the Blessed Virgin Mary, became a great promoter of the Sacred Heart devotion only after reading Saint Gertrude's works. A French edition of Gertrude's *Legatus* was published in 1671. It is possible the book was read aloud in an obscure convent in Paray-le-Monial, where a young woman named Margaret Mary Alacoque had recently become a novice.

Three

Saint Margaret Mary

As a lily among brambles, so is my love among maidens.
Song of Songs 2:2

I thank thee, Father, Lord of heaven and earth, that thou hast hidden these things from the wise and understanding and revealed them to babes; yea, Father, for such was thy gracious will.
Matthew 11:25–26

He who conquers, I will grant him to sit with me on my throne, as I myself conquered and sat down with my Father on his throne.
Revelation 3:21

Margaret Alacoque was born on the Feast of St. Mary Magdalene, July 22, 1647, in Burgundy, east central France. She was one of seven children born to Claude Alacoque and Philiberte Lamyn. Baptized Margaret two days after her birth, she added the name Mary at her confirmation in 1669 at the age of twenty-two.

Claude Alacoque worked as a royal notary and a judge. The family was well off, but even from her earliest years, Margaret found pleasure not so much in wealth or comfort but in God. She was an extraordinarily religious child, and her yearning to please God led her to take a vow of chastity when she was only four or five years old. She described these experiences in her autobiography.

> O my only Love! how much I am indebted to Thee!…From my tenderest years Thou didst prevent me with Thy grace and didst constitute Thyself the Master and possessor of my heart, although Thou knewest full well the resistance it would make Thee. As soon as I was able to know myself, Thou didst manifest to my soul the hideousness of sin, the sight of which imprinted in my heart so intense a horror thereof, that the least stain was an insupportable torment to me. In order to check my childish vivacity, it sufficed to say

that God would be offended; this would make me stop at once and turn away from what I wanted to do.

Without knowing their meaning, I felt continually urged to pronounce the following words: "O my God, I consecrate to thee my purity, and I make thee a vow of perpetual chastity." This I did once between the two elevations at Mass which I was wont to hear on my bare knees, even in the coldest weather. I did not then understand what I had done, nor what was meant by the words "vow" and "chastity."

In addition she recalled a strong bond with the Blessed Virgin Mary. "The Blessed Virgin has always taken great care of me. I had recourse to her in all my necessities, and she has preserved me from great dangers."

Margaret's father died when she was eight years old. Shortly after that, she was sent to a boarding school run by the Urbanist sisters at Charolles. She received two years of education there, which was to be the only formal schooling she would ever have. And it was at Charolles that she received the Eucharist for the first time at the age of nine. Receiving Jesus brought about a marked change in her. She became less likely to delight in the small pleasures of childhood and more drawn to prayer. Still she enjoyed her life at the convent and admired the nuns. She hoped to remain there, but a serious illness made that impossible.

> I fell, however, into so pitiable a state of ill-health that for about four years I was unable to walk, my bones piercing my skin. Consequently, I was removed from the Convent at the end of two years; but, as no remedy could be found for my illness, I was consecrated to the Blessed Virgin, with the promise that, if she cured me, I should one day be one of her daughters. Scarcely had I made this vow, than I was cured and taken anew under the protection of Our Lady. She made herself so completely Mistress of my heart, that, looking upon me as her own, she governed me as wholly dedicated to her, reproving me for my faults and teaching me how to do the Will of God.

Margaret experienced terrible conditions at home for several years because some abusive relatives moved into the house where she lived with her mother. She endured an atmosphere of persecution because these relatives were so unkind to her. The child sought refuge in mental prayer, especially prayer before the Blessed Sacrament. "I could have passed whole days and nights there, without eating or drinking, and without knowing what I was doing, except that I was being consumed in His presence like a burning taper, in order to return Him love for love. I could not remain at the entrance to the church and, in spite of the confusion I felt, I never failed to go as near as I could to the Blessed Sacrament."

Margaret's mother suffered a long illness during this time, and Margaret spent much of her time taking care of her. As Margaret grew older, her mother and other family members began to put intense pressure on her to marry. Her warmth and vivacity attracted the young men in her area, and she had many suitors. For a time she consented to meet many of the men who were interested in her to appease her mother's tearful pleas; however, she was drawn to the religious life, and she had made a vow of chastity as a child. Margaret gave herself to the Blessed Mother as her slave. She made this offering before Saint Louis de Montfort popularized the practice of "holy slavery" to Jesus through Mary. The clash between Margaret's wishes and those of her family produced a wrenching inner conflict that continued for years.

Also, the powers of hell arrayed themselves against her vocation. "Satan, too, said to me continually: 'Poor wretch, what do you mean by wishing to be a nun? You will become the laughing stock of the world, for you will never be able to persevere, and how ashamed you will be, when you put off the religious habit and leave the Convent! Where will you then go to hide yourself?'"

The maddening turmoil continued for a time, but relief came in the form of a sacrament. The bishop of the diocese where Margaret lived was often absent from the area because he was also the king's official chaplain. When a bishop from a neighboring diocese visited the region, Margaret finally had an opportunity to be confirmed. She took Mary as her confirmation name in 1669 at the age of twenty-two. Reception of the sacrament strengthened her resolve to follow the religious life, but another two years passed before she entered the convent.

Margaret Mary eventually succeeded in persuading her family that she was determined to become a nun; however, there was more conflict about when she should enter a convent and which one she should choose. Her family wanted her to enter an Ursuline convent where a cousin already lived, but she was drawn to the Visitation order. Saint Francis de Sales and Saint Jane Frances de Chantal had founded the religious institute of the Visitation of the Blessed Virgin in 1610, and Chantal was its first director.

Francis de Sales (1567–1622) was a gifted man who served the church as a priest, lawyer and writer. He became bishop of Geneva at the age of thirty-five. Francis was renowned as a preacher, and while his duties as bishop kept him busy, he made the personal direction of souls one of his highest priorities. His book, *An Introduction to the Devout Life*, is a classic devotional masterpiece that remains popular to this day. In this work he presents a way for ordinary people to reach a high degree of sanctity. He wrote several other books as well; perhaps the best known of these is his *Treatise on the Love of God*. While he didn't stress the Sacred Heart of Jesus, he did mention it in his *Treatise*.

> God's love is seated within the Savior's heart as on a royal throne. He beholds through the cleft of his pierced side all the hearts of the children of men. His heart is king of hearts, and he keeps his eyes fixed on our hearts. Just as those who peer through a lattice see clearly while they themselves are only half seen, so too the divine love within that heart, or rather that heart of divine love, always sees our hearts and looks on them with his eyes of love, while we do not see him, but only half see him. If we could see him as he is, O God, since we are mortal men we would die for love

47

of him, just as when he was in mortal flesh he died for us, and just as he would still die for us if he were not now immortal. Oh, if we could hear this divine heart singing with a voice infinitely sweet his canticle of praise to the divinity! What joy,... what striving within our heart to spring up to heaven so as to hear it forever!

We also find references to the Heart of Jesus in the writings of Saint Jane Frances de Chantal (1572–1641). She entered the religious life after her husband died and her children were grown. In this passage about prayer, she recommended complete abandonment to God.

It is in a spiritual way that God gives Himself, reaching to the deepest depths of the heart with His inspirations, and uniting Himself so gently with the soul that words cannot express what happens. The net result is that whoever is thus joined to God becomes one spirit with Him.

Let us drown ourselves then in this Ocean of holiness, of infinite purity. If we lose all, we will gain all.

I tell you for certain that the divine Heart will never fail us, if we do not fail Him. And even if we did, He would not fail us because His fidelity is greater than our unfaithfulness. He is not one of those who breaks faith with a person who has broken faith with Him, and we will always find Him ready to call us back.

Let us humble ourselves before the grandeur of God; let us make ourselves nothing in the presence of this Unknown; let us lose ourselves forever, never thinking of finding ourselves again; let us plunge into this divine abyss.

The two people who started the Visitation order had helped to erect a foundation for the modern devotion to the Sacred Heart decades before St. Margaret Mary entered the convent. In retrospect it is clear that the hand of God influenced the saint's choice of the Visitation order. But in her own mind, several factors helped her to choose. She wanted to go to a convent where she didn't know anyone so she could be solely dedicated to God's service. The Visitation order fulfilled this desire and had the added attraction of being dedicated to the Blessed Virgin Mary. And Saint Francis de Sales, who had died decades before St. Margaret Mary was born, played a role in her choice, as she related in her autobiography.

"Once when I was looking at a picture of the great Saint Francis of Sales, it seemed to me that he called me 'his daughter' and cast upon me a look so full of paternal love I no longer regarded him otherwise than as 'my good father.'"

Saint Margaret Mary made her first trip to the Visitation convent at Paray-le-Monial on May 25, 1671. As soon as she entered the parlor of the convent, she heard these words interiorly: "It is here that I would have thee to be." She left to settle her affairs in the outside world, returned to the convent the following month, and received her religious habit on August 25. God began to lavish graces on her, and she often heard His voice interiorly. She told the director of novices about these events, and as a result her superiors delayed her profession of vows because her experiences were so extraordinary. After many trials she made her profession on November 6, 1672. Her mystical experiences increased even more after she took her vows; she felt God's presence continuously and often heard Him speak to her.

On October 4, 1673, the Feast of Saint Francis of Assisi, God allowed Saint Margaret Mary to have a vision of Francis. God gave Francis to her as a guide for her soul, a guide who would lead her through the pains and trials that awaited her. A few months later, she received the first great revelation about the Sacred Heart of Jesus. This took place on December 27, the Feast of Saint

John the Evangelist. Margaret Mary described
the experience in her autobiography.

> One day, having a little more
> leisure—for the occupations con-
> fided to me left me scarcely any—I
> was praying before the Blessed
> Sacrament, when I felt myself
> wholly penetrated with that Divine
> Presence, but to such a degree that
> I lost all thought of myself and of
> the place where I was, and aban-
> doned myself to this Divine Spirit,
> yielding up my heart to the power
> of His love. He made me repose for
> a long time upon His Sacred Breast,
> where He disclosed to me the mar-
> vels of His love and the inexplicable
> secrets of His Sacred Heart, which
> so far He had concealed from me.
> Then it was that, for the first time,
> He opened to me His Divine Heart
> in a manner so real and sensible as
> to be beyond all doubt, by reason
> of the effects which this favor pro-
> duced in me, fearful, as I always am,
> of deceiving myself in anything that
> I say of what passes in me. It seems
> to me that this is what took place:
> "My Divine Heart," He said, "is so
> inflamed with love for men, and for

thee in particular that, being unable any longer to contain within Itself the flames of Its burning Charity, It must needs spread them abroad by thy means, and manifest Itself to them (mankind) in order to enrich them with the precious treasures which I discover to thee, and which contain graces of sanctification and salvation necessary to withdraw them from the abyss of perdition. I have chosen thee as an abyss of unworthiness and ignorance for the accomplishment of this great design, in order that everything may be done by Me."

After this he asked for my heart, which I begged Him to take. He did so and placed it in His own Adorable Heart where He showed it to me as a little atom which was being consumed in this great furnace, and withdrawing it thence as a burning flame in the form of a heart, He restored it to the place whence He had taken it saying to me: "See, My well-beloved, I give thee a precious token of My love, having enclosed within thy side a little spark of its glowing flames, that it may serve thee for a heart and consume thee to the last moment of thy life; its ardor will never be exhausted, and thou wilt be able to find some slight relief only by bleeding. Even this remedy I shall so mark with My Cross, that it will bring thee more humiliation and suffering than alleviation. Therefore I will that thou ask for it with simplicity, both that thou mayest practice what is ordered thee as also to give thee the consolation of shedding thy blood on the cross of humiliations. As a proof that the great favor I have done thee is not imagination, and is the foundation of all those which I intend further to confer upon thee, although I have enclosed the wound in thy side, the pain will always remain. If hitherto, thou hast taken only the name of My slave, I now give thee that of the beloved disciple of My Sacred Heart."

After such a signal favor which lasted for a long time, during which I knew not whether I was in heaven or on earth, I remained for several days, as it were, on fire and inebriated (with divine love) and so completely out of myself, that I had to

do myself violence in order to utter
a single word. The effort I had to
make in order to join in recreation
or take food was so great that it was
all I could do to overcome myself,
which was a cause of considerable
humiliation to me. I was not able to
sleep, because of the pain of the
wound, which is so precious to me;
it produces such heat within me that
it burns and consumes me alive.

Successive revelations took place the follow-
ing year, and we have several accounts of them.
One is from a letter from Saint Margaret Mary to
Father John Croiset.

I saw this divine Heart as on a
throne of flames, more brilliant than
the sun and transparent as crystal.
It had Its adorable wound and was
encircled with a crown of thorns,
which signified the pricks our sins
caused Him. It was surmounted by
a cross which signified that, from
the first moment of His Incarnation,
that is, from the time this Sacred
Heart was formed, the cross was
planted in It; that it was filled, from
the very first moment, with all the
bitterness, humiliations, poverty,

sorrow, and contempt His sacred
humanity would have to suffer during the whole course of His life and
during His holy Passion.

He made me understand that
the ardent desire He had of being
loved by men and of drawing them
from the path of perdition into
which Satan was hurrying them in
great numbers, had caused Him
to fix upon this plan of manifesting
His Heart to men, together with all
Its treasures of love, mercy, grace,
sanctification and salvation. This He
did in order that those who were
willing to do all in their power to
render and procure for Him honor,
love, and glory might be enriched
abundantly, even profusely, with
these divine treasures of the Heart
of God, which is their source. It
must be honored under the symbol
of this Heart of flesh, whose image
He wished to be publicly exposed.
He wanted me to carry it on my
person, over my heart, that He
might imprint His love there, fill my
heart with all the gifts with which
His own is filled, and destroy all
inordinate affection. Wherever this
sacred image would be exposed for

veneration He would pour forth His graces and blessings. This devotion was as a last effort of His love which wished to favor men in these last centuries with this loving redemption, in order to withdraw them from the empire of Satan, which He intended to destroy, and in order to put us under the sweet liberty of the empire of His love. This He would establish in the hearts of all those who would embrace this devotion.

After this, the Sovereign of my soul said to me: "These are the designs for which I have chosen you. That is why I have given you so many graces and have taken quite special care of you from your very cradle. I Myself have been your teacher and your director only that I might prepare you for the accomplishment of this great design and confide to you this great treasure which I am displaying to you here." Then, prostrating myself on the ground, I exclaimed with St. Thomas, "My Lord and my God!" I find it impossible to express what I felt on that occasion. I did not know whether I was in heaven or on earth.

On another day during that year, Jesus appeared to Saint Margaret Mary as she was praying before the Blessed Sacrament. He asked her to adopt certain practices to make reparation to His Sacred Heart for her sins and those of others. Jesus asked her to begin keeping a Holy Hour on Thursday nights in honor of his suffering in the Garden of Olives. He also asked her to begin receiving Communion on the first Friday of each month. This was an important turning point because God had prevented her from speaking about the apparitions until then. The circumstances of this apparition and the results they produced in the saint forced her to speak about her experiences. Saint Margaret Mary was overwhelmed with graces during the apparition. "I lost all consciousness during that time and I no longer knew where I was. When they came to withdraw me, seeing that I could make no reply, nor even stand except with great difficulty, they led me to Our Mother (Mother Marie-Francoise de Saumaise)."

Margaret Mary wasn't free to adopt these practices of making a Holy Hour and receiving Communion on first Fridays without getting permission from Mother de Saumaise. The superior initially refused, believing it would be unwise to allow practices that deviated from the norms of convent life. Margaret Mary then became so ill with a succession of fevers that a doctor called in to treat her believed she would die. Mother de Saumaise responded to this crisis by telling Margaret Mary to pray and ask God to restore her health. If good health returned, the superior would interpret it as a sign that the apparitions were from God. Margaret Mary asked God to heal her, and He restored her to health immediately. Thus, she received permission to keep the Holy Hour on Thursday nights and receive Communion on first Fridays.

While Margaret Mary delighted in receiving permission to make these changes, this period was one of severe trials for her. Mother de Saumaise asked the saint to speak to some theologians about what was taking place within her. They failed to recognize the divine nature of these events, telling her to resist unusual experiences. In addition God sometimes asked her to pass messages to the other sisters in the convent, which she did in the form of notes. She might give one sister a note saying that God wanted her to be more fervent in prayer. Then she might tell another sister that God wanted her to be more charitable.

At the time the other sisters were unaware of the apparitions. All they knew was that they had an inexperienced sister who seemed arrogant in correcting her elders. And they suspected she had hoodwinked the superior into letting her adopt some strange new practices. Margaret

Mary became an unpopular woman in her convent. She asked God to help her, and He said He would. "He would send me his faithful servant and perfect friend," she wrote, "who would teach me to know Him and to abandon myself to Him without further resistance."

Saint Claude de la Colombiere (1641–1682), a brilliant Jesuit, soon arrived at Paray and become confessor to the Visitation sisters. Saint Margaret Mary described meeting Father Claude in 1675 in a letter written years later. "What showed me clearly the will of God at this meeting was that the good Father asked for me quite spontaneously without our having known each other, and at the same time I heard these words spoken clearly within me: 'This is he whom I send you.'"

At that time and in following meetings, she described what had been taking place within her. Saint Claude asked her to begin keeping a journal of these experiences. Also, he told her to yield to the power of God. "After this good Father had come to know all that had taken place in me, he forbade me ever to resist this spirit. I must abandon myself completely to His good pleasure and let Him act in me to the full extent of His power. This brought me unalterable peace of soul."

Just a few months later, in June of 1675, Saint Margaret Mary received the last of the great revelations of the Sacred Heart, which she recounted in her autobiography.

Being before the Blessed Sacrament one day of Its octave, I received from my God signal tokens of His love, and felt urged with the desire of making Him some return, and of rendering love for love. "Thou canst not make me a greater return of love," He said, "than by doing what I have so often asked of thee." Then discovering to me His Divine Heart, He said: "Behold this Heart, Which has loved men so much, that It has spared nothing, even to exhausting and consuming Itself, in order to testify to them Its love; and in return I receive from the greater number nothing but ingratitude by reason of their irreverence and sacrileges, and by the coldness and contempt they show Me in this Sacrament of Love. But what I feel the most keenly is that it is hearts which are consecrated to Me, that treat Me thus. Therefore, I ask of thee that the Friday after the Octave of Corpus Christi be set apart for a special Feast to honor My Heart, by communicating on that day and making reparation to It by a solemn act, in order to make amends for the indignities which

It has received during the time It
has been exposed on the altars. I
promise thee that My Heart shall
expand Itself to shed in abundance
the influence of Its divine love upon
those who shall thus honor It, and
cause It to be honored."

Saint Margaret Mary then told Jesus that she
didn't know how to carry out this task. Jesus said
she should work with Saint Claude to do it. The
two saints consecrated themselves to the Sacred
Heart of Jesus during that month. Both spent the
rest of their lives promoting the devotion. Father
Claude was sent to England the following year.
He was often in danger, and was imprisoned for a
time because of the persecution of Catholics taking place then. Yet he faithfully preached about
the Sacred Heart of Jesus. Saint Margaret Mary
spent years praying for the spread of the devotion, although it was not practiced in her convent.

By 1678 Saint Margaret Mary was writing letters to members of her order in other convents
who had heard of this "new" devotion in one way
or another and wanted to know more about it.
Her correspondents eventually included members of other orders, priests and lay people. More
than one hundred of these letters have been preserved, and they form a rich source of information about the devotion as it was revealed to the
saint. Their immediate effect was to spread the

devotion to an ever-widening circle of friends, relatives and even strangers. In these letters we find the themes that have become foundations of the modern devotion to the Sacred Heart.

Margaret Mary emphasized love and charity for God and neighbor, including the souls in purgatory. She wrote of the need for repentance and reparation. Other themes include God's merciful love for sinners, a formal consecration to the Sacred Heart and abandonment to God's will. Margaret Mary stressed a deep reverence for, and devotion to, the Passion and a tender love for Jesus in the Eucharist. Many people who knew about the devotion, however, still regarded it as a dangerous novelty. Members of the Visitation order didn't openly practice the devotion; it was still a strictly private affair.

Saint Claude returned from England and spent some time at Paray, dying there of tuberculosis on February 15, 1682. It appeared as though Saint Margaret Mary lost her most fervent ally, but Father Claude continued playing a notable role in her life. Years later Margaret Mary advised a priest, who was working on spreading the devotion, to pray to Jesus and Father Claude. "We must go to His faithful friend, the good Father de la Colombiere, to whom He has given great power and in whose hands He has placed, so to speak, everything that concerns this devotion. I tell you confidentially that I have received great help from him, more now even than when he was here on earth. For this devotion to the Sacred Heart, if I am not mistaken, has made him very powerful in heaven and has brought him a higher degree of glory than anything else he could have done during his entire life."

The first public honor rendered to the Sacred Heart in the convent at Paray occurred in 1685. Saint Margaret Mary served as director of novices that year. The novices had been preparing a celebration for her in honor of her feast day (the Feast of Saint Margaret, July 20). The feast fell on a Friday, and Margaret Mary convinced her novices to forgo paying any honor to her. The group held a celebration in honor of the Sacred Heart instead. They arranged an altar, placed an ink sketching representing the Sacred Heart on it and said prayers in honor of the Sacred Heart. Their actions resulted in an outburst of criticism from some of the other sisters. They again accused Margaret Mary of trying to introduce a new devotion.

A sweeping change took place early the following year when Saint Claude's sermons and retreat notes were published. The retreat notes were filled with references to the Sacred Heart of Jesus. They also mentioned that Father Claude knew someone who had experienced visions of the Sacred Heart. Many people realized this must be a reference to Sister Margaret Mary, and their attitudes toward her and the devotion changed dramatically. In June of 1686, almost fifteen years after the first great revelation to Saint Margaret Mary, members of the Visitation community at Paray celebrated the feast of the Sacred Heart together. Saint Claude's writings and Saint Margaret Mary's letters helped to spread the devotion to other convents of the Visitation order and eventually to the entire world.

Saint Margaret Mary spent the final years of her life exulting in the spread of the devotion and begging Jesus to pour out the blessings of His Sacred Heart on humanity. In her letters she often wrote about the value of consecrating one's life to the Sacred Heart and following Jesus in the way of virtue. She stressed charity, humility, reverence for the Passion, embracing the cross in whatever way God offers it, and conformity to God's will. The saint explained that people who practiced the devotion and struggled to gain these virtues would receive a torrent of graces from the Heart of Jesus. These graces would help them to reach a degree of sanctity that would otherwise be almost impossible.

Love and charity form the foundation of this devotion, and for Margaret Mary, love of God and love of one's neighbors were inseparable. She urged people to remember the souls in purgatory, whose suffering is reduced when those who are consecrated to the Sacred Heart pray for them. In several letters Margaret Mary described how God would sometimes allow her to communicate with souls in purgatory, who found relief from their suffering because of the prayers and sacrifices she offered for them. In one instance she described how some souls she had been praying for were being released from purgatory. "They were taken up midst songs of inexpressible joy." Then she added, "As I was begging them not to forget us they said to me these parting words: 'Ingratitude has never yet entered heaven.'"

In 1689 Saint Margaret Mary began corresponding with John Croiset, a Jesuit priest. These letters about the Sacred Heart devotion were lengthy and detailed. She noted that she was taking the time to write them because Jesus had told her that Father Croiset had been chosen to become a promoter of the devotion. The time had come for her to pass on much of what had been revealed to her. She died the following year on October 17, 1690.

Saint Margaret Mary's contribution to establishing and spreading the modern devotion to the Sacred Heart cannot be overstated. The devotion, which saints and mystics had treasured since the time of Saint John the Evangelist, was conveyed to the whole world through this extraordinary woman. She fervently embraced the crosses involved in spreading the devotion. Her efforts gave ordinary people many practical ways (such as receiving Communion on first Fridays) to approach the Heart of Jesus, with its fiery love, ineffable tenderness and infinite treasures. Almost every major revelation of the

Sacred Heart to Saint Margaret Mary took place in a Eucharistic setting, and Jesus urged her and others to receive Communion as often as possible. These revelations occurred during an era when certain factions in the church discouraged the frequent reception of Communion, and the revelations helped to check this insidious trend.

In 1691, just a year after Saint Margaret Mary's death, Father John Croiset published *The Devotion to the Sacred Heart of Jesus.* Margaret Mary had told Father Croiset that God Himself had inspired him to write the book, which became a success and was translated into many languages. This classic work on the devotion is still available in English. Father Croiset's book and the writings of Saint Claude and Saint Margaret Mary helped to fuel the spread of the devotion. However, the actions of the millions of Catholics who consecrated themselves to the Sacred Heart and experienced His infinite blessings firsthand have produced wave after wave of interest in the devotion for centuries. Jesus has often granted healings to those who honor His Sacred Heart. Many such miracles go unnoticed by the world at large, but these blessings became public in 1720 when a plague struck the city of Marseilles in France, killing about forty thousand people. The bishop and other city leaders consecrated the city to the Sacred Heart, and citizens were asked to join in processions through the streets while reciting litanies and other prayers to the

Sacred Heart of Jesus. This massive outpouring of prayers mounted up to heaven, and Jesus responded by stopping the plague instantly.

A Mass and Office for the Feast of the Sacred Heart were approved for Poland at the request of the Polish bishops in 1765, and the feast was extended to the universal church in 1856. The popes have issued various documents to encourage the spread of the devotion, ranging from lengthy encyclicals to a series of meditations on the Litany of the Sacred Heart written by Pope John Paul II. A thorough survey of papal documents related to the devotion can be found in Timothy T. O'Donnell's excellent book, *Heart of the Redeemer*.

Saint Margaret Mary's canonization in 1920 helped to spark renewed interest in the devotion as a growing number of people became familiar with her life. Many have been attracted to the devotion because of her writings, particularly her descriptions of the flood of blessings Jesus showers on those who honor His Heart. These blessings have become known as the promises of the Sacred Heart.

Four

The Splendor of Carmel

With zeal I have been zealous for
the Lord God of hosts.
    1 Kings 19:10, The Carmelite Seal

Therefore, behold, I will allure her,
and bring her into the wilderness,
and speak tenderly to her.
    Hosea 2:14

God is love, and he who abides in
love abides in God, and God abides
in him.
    1 John 4:16

Even before a liturgical feast honoring the
Sacred Heart of Jesus was established, the
devotion spread rapidly. In a movement that
would be repeated centuries later, when millions

of Catholics honored Jesus in a special way on Divine Mercy Sunday before the Church officially established the feast, lay people adopted the Sacred Heart devotion in their homes and parishes. The devotion spread from France to other countries, largely because of efforts made by members of the Society of Jesus.

The sacred fire was now to take a different hue. Jesus had previously called certain people, such as Saint Gertrude and Saint Margaret Mary, to extraordinary sanctity through the devotion. His revelations had come in the form of startling visions and transforming locutions. Now He wanted to make these inebriating graces, previously and primarily reserved to great mystics and visionaries, available to everyone. Ordinary people would find a path to holiness simply by embracing devotion to the Sacred Heart. No extraordinary visions were necessary. Jesus carried out His designs in silence in the ordinary details of everyday life, granting graces of sanctification to people of goodwill who surrendered their hearts to Him.

Devotion to the Sacred Heart spread rapidly from its stronghold in monastic communities to the laity. Individuals and families embraced Jesus in a new way as the devotion spread. Children learned of the Sacred Heart while they were still young, and their devotion would become a foundational part of their spiritual lives, which blossomed as they became teenagers and adults. They would continue honoring Jesus through

His Heart as they married and formed families of their own. Those who had religious vocations would already have a deep devotion to the Sacred Heart when they entered religious life. As it happened, some of the most ardent lovers of the Sacred Heart would eventually enter the Carmelite order.

Ignatius Redi, a resident of Arezzo, may have been among the first Italian laypeople to embrace the Sacred Heart of Jesus. His brother, Diego Redi, was a Jesuit priest who was deeply attached to the devotion, even composing hymns in honor of the Sacred Heart. Ignatius and his wife, Camilla, had thirteen children. Their second child, Anna Maria, the future Saint Teresa Margaret of the Sacred Heart of Jesus, was born on July 15, 1747. She was baptized the following day, on the Feast of Our Lady of Mount Carmel.

The young Anna Maria had a precocious interest in God and often asked her father penetrating questions about God as they strolled to Mass together. The two of them developed an unusually intimate relationship, and she absorbed a deep devotion to the Sacred Heart from her father. Anna lived at home during her early years, but after her ninth birthday, she started attending a boarding school run by the Benedictine sisters of Saint Apollonia's in Florence. She would stay at the school until 1764, when her formal education was complete. During these years she came to love living in a building where the Blessed Sacrament was reserved and developed an attraction for the religious life but not to any particular religious order.

During this era girls who had a vocation to the religious life followed a custom of making a series of farewell visits to friends and family before entering a convent. In September of 1763, Cecilia Albergotti, a girl from Arezzo who was a friend of Anna Maria's, paid such a visit to Saint Apollonia's in Florence. Cecilia knew some of the sisters at Saint Apollonia's as well as Anna Maria. Cecilia was about to enter the Carmelite monastery in Florence, where she would become Sister Teresa of Jesus Crucified.

Anna Maria met her friend and chatted warmly with her in the parlor. Then, just after Cecilia's departure, Anna Maria heard a heavenly voice speaking to her. "I am Teresa of Jesus, and I want you among my daughters." Saint Teresa of Avila herself, the great founder of the Discalced branch of the Carmelite order, was speaking to her. Anna Maria was surprised and upset because she wasn't accustomed to locutions, and she didn't know how to interpret the experience. She fled to the chapel to spend time before the Blessed Sacrament, her habitual refuge in times of distress. There she heard the same voice. "I am Teresa of Jesus, and I tell you that in a short time you shall be in my monastery."

While drawn to the religious life, Anna Maria, who was only sixteen years old, had never seriously considered Carmel before. She didn't have a spiritual director and initially told no one of the word she had received from heaven. The following spring she completed her formal studies at Saint Apollonia's and returned to her family home in Arezzo. By that time she was already eager to enter Carmel, but her father (who still didn't know about her Carmelite vocation) had told her ahead of time that she was too young to decide on a vocation. He wanted her to wait, at least until her seventeenth birthday in July.

Her months in Arezzo were full of activity and a longing for solitude. Camilla was sick at the time, so Anna Maria helped her mother by caring for her younger brothers and sisters. She also had an active social life at her parent's bidding. While she treated others with kindness and respect, she longed to withdraw from the world to spend more time in prayer and slipped away when she could. During this time she placed herself under the spiritual direction of Father Jerome Gioni, a Jesuit. Without guidance from her parents, she may have withdrawn from the world during this time, and she wanted to adopt a radically plain style of dress that would have been distinctive for a girl her age.

But Father Gioni told her to be obedient to her parents' wishes about social activities and dress. As a result Anna Maria learned to be in the world but not of it—to continue dressing like everyone else. She blended in seamlessly in a way that didn't call attention to herself. This manner of being eventually blossomed into a distinctive spirituality. Anna Maria lived a hidden life out in the open. She didn't stand out in a crowd but mirrored the hidden life of Jesus. This quiet blending in with others became one of the hallmarks of her spiritual life. She was so successful that many who knew her, including those who lived with her, didn't suspect she was reaching extraordinary spiritual heights.

On her seventeenth birthday Anna Maria told her mother about her desire to enter Carmel. Her choice astounded her family; Ignatius Redi was torn. While he wanted Anna Maria to be free to follow her true vocation, he knew that having this lovable daughter in a cloistered community would be difficult for him. He asked her to speak to her spiritual director and several other priests, including the provincial of the Tuscan province of the Discalced Carmelites, who happened to be visiting Arezzo. The priests discerned that her vocation to Carmel was indeed authentic. She wrote a letter to the superior of the Carmel in Florence, seeking permission to come to the convent, and received a warm response.

Anna Maria arrived at the Carmelite monastery in Florence, accompanied by her father, on September 1, 1764. Many of the sisters chose a religious name that was different from their name in the world. Anna Maria said she would be happy to keep her family name, but there was already a Sister Anna Maria in the community. She told the superior she would like to take the founder's name. But it is a rare Carmelite community that doesn't already have a Sister Teresa. Anna Maria then suggested that she combine Teresa with Margaret after Sister Margaret Mary, who was starting to become known as the great promoter of the Sacred Heart devotion. So it was that Anna Maria temporarily took the name of Sister Teresa Margaret on her first day in Carmel.

She spent several months as a postulant, left briefly, following a local custom, and then returned to become a novice. It is at this time that a sister takes the simple, brown Carmelite habit and finalizes her religious name. In March 1765 she received the habit and her full religious name: Sister Teresa Margaret of the Sacred Heart of Jesus.

The superior later said that Teresa Margaret suffered because of the separation from her family, especially her father, but accepted the suffering as part of her vocation. Intense fervor marked her novitiate. During this period she met Father Ildephonse, who became her spiritual director and one of only a few people who recognized the extraordinary sanctity of this young woman during her lifetime.

Just as she was starting the novitiate, her father gave her a copy of a biography of the then

Venerable Margaret Mary. While Sister Teresa Margaret had grown up in a home where the Sacred Heart devotion was warmly practiced, the book, which contained extensive quotes from Margaret Mary, had a great impact on Carmel's newest novice. Teresa Margaret decided to take Margaret Mary as her "novice-mistress" and absorbed all she could of her model and mentor.

Her devotion to the Heart of Jesus deepened and matured as she read and reread the biography. Sometimes she would quote Margaret Mary word for word in letters, and she got to know her work so well that she could even quote passages from it during conversations. The mysterious journey of her soul into the Heart of the Eternal Word reached new peaks of intensity and fervor, and she became aflame with love. Nonetheless, her attachment to the hidden life of Jesus, exemplified by the silent determination of her predecessor Margaret Mary, guided her spiritual life. She would remain largely unnoticed. Members of her community would occasionally catch a glimmer of the radiant light that was transforming the soul of their sister. But her efforts to ensure that she blended into the common life of her community, remaining unremarkable, veiled her extraordinary love for Jesus from others.

Father Ildephonse would later write that Sister Teresa Margaret regarded the Sacred Heart as "the center of the love of the Divine Word, Who loved us from all eternity in the bosom of the

Father and Who, thanks to this same love, has obtained for us the ability to love Him in return, both on earth and in heaven, by participating in His love. This is the meaning which…I find that she gave to this devotion, making it consist completely in loving in return the One Who has first loved us."

At her profession Teresa Margaret took another radical and painful step on the path to sanctity. Fearing that her close relationship with her father might not be fully in accord with God's will, she wrote to Ignatius and told him she was detaching herself from him to belong to Jesus. She explained that she wanted her future contacts with him to be purely spiritual in nature or prompted by obedience to her superiors. She suggested, however, that they continue to meet every evening "in the Heart of Jesus." Ignatius responded by writing a letter, graciously accepting his daughter's proposal.

Carmelite sisters spend hours in prayer every day and observe silence much of the time. The daily routine of work, prayer and silence was perfect for Sister Teresa Margaret. She simply followed the rhythms of daily life in the community without drawing attention to herself even as she became aflame with an extraordinary love for Jesus. But an incident during her novitiate betrayed how love was transforming her.

Sister Teresa Margaret worked as a server in the refectory, where the sisters took meals together. Her duties forced her to wait until everyone else had eaten before she was able to take the meal herself. One day everyone had left except Sister Mary Victoria of the Trinity. Sister Mary Victoria had suffered extraordinary intermittent pains from toothaches since she was a child and often took longer to eat than everyone else.

Sister Teresa Margaret noticed that her companion was eating slowly and crying in silence because of the pain from her tooth. She rose, went over to her, said a few comforting words, and impulsively kissed her on the cheek. (In so doing, she managed to simultaneously break two of the community's rules by breaking silence and failing to show physical reserve with the other sisters). The pain left Sister Mary Victoria immediately, never to return. The two sisters reported the incident to their superior, who was obligated to reprimand Sister Teresa Margaret for breaking the community's rules. Still, all three sisters knew this miraculous kiss had been a vehicle of God's love as He extended His healing touch through Sister Teresa Margaret.

With the notable exception of this spontaneous kiss, Sister Teresa Margaret followed the community rule scrupulously and asked permission before doing anything out of the ordinary. On one occasion she asked Father Ildephonse for permission to write a short resolution to Jesus in her own blood. He gave her permission to do so as long as she kept the resolution very short to avoid excessive bleeding. She never mentioned the resolution again. After her death the sisters found the resolution among the papers in her cell, the words written in no ordinary ink, because they were of a brownish hue. "My Jesus I am determined to be all yours, whatever the cost, and despite every repugnance."

One Sunday in 1767, while reciting the Divine Office, Sister Teresa Margaret heard these words from the First Epistle of John: "God is love, and he who dwells in love dwells in God, and God in him." While she had heard these words many times before, on this day a deep illumination that intensified her desire to become one with God accompanied them. Teresa Margaret, who normally avoided drawing attention to herself, surprised several of the sisters in the following days as she repeated the words "God is love" with great wonder and expressiveness. (The sisters recited the prayers in Latin, so she heard "Deus caritas est." Centuries later, Pope Benedict XVI would choose these words for the name of his first encyclical). The graces she received then intensified her desire to abide in God. At the same time, her desire to love God expressed itself in practical service to members of her community. She asked for more duties, especially caring for the sick sisters in the infirmary, including one sister who was difficult to care for because of a serious mental illness.

Meanwhile, Sister Teresa Margaret cared for others who were sick. One of her patients was elderly and almost deaf, yet she understood everything Teresa Margaret said to her, even when she spoke in a soft voice. And Sister Teresa Margaret also had a knack for knowing when one of her patients needed her.

Carmel is the divine desert, and Teresa Margaret also had experiences of great spiritual darkness, dryness in prayer and distaste for all things holy, which tormented her even as her trials were sanctifying her. During a retreat in 1768, she wrote out a series of resolutions she wanted to follow. Then, consumed by her love for Jesus, she wrote out the following act of complete oblation: "My God, I do not want anything else other than to become a perfect image of You and, because Your life was a hidden life of humiliation, love, and sacrifice, I desire the same for myself. I wish, therefore, to enclose myself in Your loving Heart as in a desert in order to live in You, with You, and for You this hidden life of love and sacrifice. You know indeed that I desire to be a victim of Your Sacred Heart, completely consumed as a holocaust by the fire of Your holy love."

Sister Teresa Margaret then entered a great spiritual battle as she struggled against various temptations. In November 1769 she wrote to Father Ildephonse about her state of soul. "Sometimes I feel the greatest repugnance for performing even the least act of virtue, and I have to do myself the greatest violence in order to perform the act; at other times I want nothing else than to conform myself perfectly with the Heart of Jesus, and then I force myself to practice those virtues that I know will make me especially beloved of that Heart."

On March 4, 1770, Sister Teresa Margaret asked Father Ildephonse for permission to make a special, general confession, and he agreed. She received Communion the next day. On the evening of March 6, after tending to several sisters in the infirmary, she was seized with sharp abdominal pains and was unable to return to her cell on her own. Several sisters helped her, and she asked them to pray the "Glory be" in honor of the Sacred Heart five times. A doctor was called, but he didn't think her condition was serious. She spent the night in agonizing pain. The following day a doctor ordered a bleeding (the all-purpose cure of that era), which appeared to relieve her pain temporarily. In the afternoon Saint Teresa Margaret spent her time holding a crucifix, kissing it, and gazing at an image of the Sacred Heart. She died around three o'clock on March 7, 1770, at the age of twenty-two.

Saint Teresa Margaret's suffering and death left her body terribly discolored, and the community planned a quick funeral. But the sisters were astonished to discover that her body changed, regaining a natural, healthy look and complete flexibility; it remained that way for days and then weeks. The bishop of Florence, accompanied by doctors, visited the monastery to view the miraculously preserved body, which remains incorrupt.

Saint Teresa Margaret was canonized in 1931. Mysteriously, this great saint of Carmel, who strove to remain hidden and unnoticed in life, remains little known to this day.

While the Sacred Heart devotion spread through Europe in the years following the death of Saint Margaret Mary, her homeland continued to be a center of the devotion for some years. When the French Revolution erupted in 1789, the devotion, in its modern form, had a deep influence on French spirituality as religious and laypeople alike integrated it into their everyday lives. Special Masses and prayers graced the first Friday of the month, but the devotion also worked its way into the fabric of Catholic culture through hymns, poetry and many works of art portraying Jesus and His Sacred Heart. With the outbreak of the revolution, a diabolical wave of secularism and hostility toward the Church engulfed France. Government authorities seized many monasteries, exiled certain priests and nuns, and took various other measures designed to "protect" the public from the alleged darkness of Christianity while imposing supposedly enlightened ideas.

A small group of Carmelite sisters in Compiegne, led by the remarkable prioress Blessed Teresa of Saint Augustine, tried to carry on normal community life despite all the obstacles. Sometimes the community made compromises to preserve its life as much as possible while still following the increasing number of laws that restricted religious activities. For example, Sister Constance, a novice and the youngest of the sisters, would normally have taken her final vows on December 15, 1789. However, in October of that year, the government issued a rule temporarily forbidding anyone from taking religious vows. Sister Constance remained in the community nonetheless.

The rule was among the first in a series of anti-Christian laws. In November of 1789 the French government declared that all Church property now belonged to the state, not the Church, and ordered an inventory of its new properties. In February of 1790 the government announced that the ban on vows would be permanent. In August government authorities descended on the Compiegne monastery to take an inventory and privately interview each sister to see how many of them wanted to return to "normal" life. All of them declined the opportunity. Meanwhile, the government agreed to give pensions to vowed religious as compensation for seized property.

In November of 1791 the legislature passed a decree requiring all clergy to swear a civic loyalty oath. In December the king of France vetoed this measure, but many local officials ignored the veto and forced people to take the oath. Then in 1792 came a decree that made wearing religious

habits in public illegal. The government chose
April 6, which was Good Friday that year, to
issue the decree. On that Easter Sunday, Mother
Teresa of Saint Augustine shared with her community the text of a mystical vision a lay woman
who had stayed at the Compiegne Carmel in the
previous century had recorded. The text was in
the community's archives. After the vision the
woman became a novice and eventually made
her profession as Sister Marie Elisabeth Baptiste.
Recorded in 1693, the vision involved Jesus and
a seemingly heavenly place.

> There I saw the glory that the
> nuns of this convent would have
> and which appeared very great and
> exalted. I saw an angel placing the
> members of the whole community.
> What surprised me was to see that
> many of the young ones were more
> elevated in glory than many of the
> older ones. I saw there several sis-
> ters I did not know, but whom I rec-
> ognized afterward. It seemed to me
> that there was a Lamb at a higher
> level, who looked at us all very lov-
> ingly. I immediately felt I was his
> and, after a long time, he looked at
> me with eyes brimming with love.
> He seemed to be giving me little
> caresses, and I saw him do as much

for all the community. As the angel was placing us I noted that he had had two or three sisters, one of whom I recognized, pass over to the other side, and I greatly feared being of their number, since I understood perfectly that they were not to follow the Lamb, and I so wanted to follow him. These two or three sisters he directed to another place, in another part of heaven. As I'd not yet been placed I strongly feared being one of them. And in that very same instance I felt myself transported with the community clothed in a white mantle and a great black veil that I did not have before and that delighted me.

After the reading of this text on that Easter Sunday, the sisters then discussed the possible implications of the call to "follow the Lamb" and that it could even involve martyrdom.

In August the government ordered the closing of all women's monasteries. Local authorities carried out the order the following month. Government officials forced the sisters out of their cloister on September 14, the Feast of the Exaltation of the Holy Cross. Several of the sisters hadn't left the monastery for fifty years. The sisters had obtained ordinary clothing from sympathetic laypeople for their departure because wearing religious habits in public was illegal. Because of the size of the community—there were twenty sisters in all—there was no place for them to stay together, and doing so would have been illegal anyway because of a law designed to break up communities. So the sisters divided themselves into four groups and found housing in local apartments laypeople made available.

The sisters tried to follow the Carmelite rule as much as possible despite their dislocation and scattering. And during the first few months, they were able to attend a daily Mass a parish priest celebrated, but a local resident denounced him for remaining faithful to the Church; he was forced to leave the country. After that the sisters were occasionally able to attend a Mass a visiting priest celebrated. Sometime during their first months in exile from their monastery, Mother Teresa of Saint Augustine proposed that the community start offering a daily prayer of consecration, in which they would offer themselves as a holocaust to the Lord to bring blessings of peace down on the French Church and the country as a whole. After some early hesitation, the sisters agreed.

The sisters spent almost two years living outside their monastery. One of them died during this period. Meanwhile, the violence of revolutionary France became even more pronounced. In September of 1793 the country entered a phase that would later become known as the Reign of Terror. The government imprisoned thousands of people. Mass executions by guillotine became a brutal, everyday reality as fanatical agents of the revolution executed thousands of people accused of opposing the government.

Sometime during this period, the sisters decided to add some more petitions to their daily prayer of consecration, specifically for freedom for prisoners and a lessening of the executions. While the violence affected many regions, Paris was the center of destruction. The upheavals displaced many families, and in March of 1794 three sisters received permission to leave Compiegne for a time to help family members elsewhere. In June Mother Teresa of Saint Augustine's Carmelite superior learned of Teresa's family situation and ordered her to take such a trip to help her elderly mother, who was preparing to leave Paris to escape the violence and upheavals there. During her time there, Mother Teresa witnessed wagonloads of prisoners being carried down the street on the way to their deaths at the guillotine.

Mother Teresa of Saint Augustine returned to Compiegne on June 21, only to discover that the police were searching all the apartments where the nuns lived. The following day all sixteen members of the community were arrested and imprisoned in a former Visitation monastery that had been converted into a jail for political prisoners. The sisters were shocked to learn that among their fellow prisoners were seventeen English Benedictine sisters who had been arrested at their convent in Cambrai and imprisoned in Compiegne since September of 1792.

Compiegne's Revolutionary Surveillance Committee sent the "evidence" it had gathered during the search of the apartments on to Paris, asking that the sisters be tried for their crimes there. On July 12 the Carmelite sisters, who had only one set of clothing apiece, were granted permission to return to their monastery for a few hours to use the laundry there. They changed into their habits and washed their other clothing. On this day the mayor of Compiegne received a response to his request to Paris, ordering the sisters to be sent there for their trial. Rather than delay their departure for a day while waiting for their soaking wet civilian clothing to dry out, the mayor ordered them to leave immediately, sur-rounded by armed guards.

The sisters spent several days in the Paris prison. On July 16, the Feast of Our Lady of Mount Carmel, they were told that their trial would take place the following day. On the morning of July 17, the sisters went to their trial. The official accu-sations against them accused them of fanaticism and referred to "evidence" seized in Compiegne, including "hearts, which are a sign of rebellion in the Vendee, fanatical and childish objects." Indeed, the hearts referred to were artistic rep-resentations of the hearts of Jesus and Mary, which were popular among faithful Catholics in the Vendee region of France. Many Catholics there openly opposed the antireligious excesses of the French Revolution. The sisters, who had nothing to do with the Vendee uprising, found themselves accused of crimes in part because they had images of the Sacred Heart of Jesus. Another piece of evidence the state offered was a hymn one of the sisters had composed. It read in part,

> Let that Heart, the world's salvation,
> By which Satan was crushed,
> Appear in the midst of thunder
> In the midst of the blazing sky!
> At its sweet and terrible appearance
> I see the factious grow pale.
> France shall then have peace,
> Her King be free, her people happy.

While Mother Teresa of Saint Augustine tried to persuade the tribunal that she alone was responsible for any "crimes" the community had committed, the sisters were all found guilty and sentenced to death. The sixteen sisters were among forty people to be executed that day.

While the mass executions of that period now strike many people as ghoulish, the revolution enjoyed much popular support. Many residents of Paris knew that those condemned to death would be taken in open carts to their place of execution late in the day. Often mobs would come out along the route to ridicule and jeer at the prisoners. This day was to be different.

Because of the ban on religious dress, it would have been a long time since residents of Paris had seen nuns in their habits. The usually unruly crowd along the route fell into silence. They beheld sisters in religious habits, radiant with joy, singing hymns and chanting prayers. The sisters sang the Miserere. Following the Carmelite rule, they chanted Vespers and later, Compline. And they sang the *Salve Regina*. Somewhere along the route a girl, Therese Binard, approached the passing carts expectantly. One of the sisters reached out, handing Binard her copy of the Divine Office. Years later Binard would become the foundress of a convent.

As the sisters made their approach to the guillotine, they praised God with the words of the *Te Deum*. Then, once out of the carts, they sang the *Veni Creator Spiritus*. The sisters then gathered around Mother Teresa of Saint Augustine and renewed their vows. So it was that Sister Constance, twenty-nine, the youngest member of the community, whom French law had prevented for years from taking her final vows, made her perpetual profession as a Carmelite at the foot of the guillotine. She was to be the first to die. But she had just taken a vow of obedience to her superior.

Defying the authority of the state and its executioners, Sister Constance knelt before Mother

Teresa of Saint Augustine and asked, "Permission to die, Mother?" Her saintly superior replied, "Go, my daughter!" She arose. Then, as she started up the steps, Sister Constance praised God by singing the first line of Psalm 117, "*Laudate Dominum Omnes Gentes.*" The community joined her in the song. Each sister in her turn asked permission to die before mounting the scaffold. The singing continued throughout the executions, diminishing one voice at a time as the guillotine blade descended. Mother Teresa of Saint Augustine was the last to die.

A further upheaval swept through France in the following days. Robespierre, who had been the chief architect of the Reign of Terror, was executed on July 28, and another mass execution took place the following day. The Reign of Terror ended that month, and peace was gradually restored to France. The daily prayer of consecration the sisters had offered bore fruit after Jesus allowed them to be martyred—in part, for their devotion to His Sacred Heart.

France, the birthplace of the modern Sacred Heart devotion, was also privileged to become the birthplace of one of the greatest saints of all time: Therese Martin of Lisieux. Therese was born on January 2, 1873, to a devout Catholic family in France at a time when the Sacred Heart devotion was flourishing. She was the youngest of nine children, four of whom died during childhood. Of the five surviving sisters, four, including Therese, became Carmelite nuns, while the fifth joined the Visitation order.

Therese would become known as the Little Flower only after her death at the age of twenty-four in 1897. Her autobiography, *Story of a Soul*, was first published in 1898. The book recounts her idyllic childhood, marred by her mother's premature death when Therese was only four years old, her early call to Carmel and the obstacles she faced when she tried to get permission to enter the order as a teenager. She gives an account of a family pilgrimage to Rome when she was fourteen years old, where she famously begged Pope Leo XIII to let her enter Carmel at the age of fifteen. He (just as famously) told her it would happen if it was God's will and left the decision up to local Church officials. Within a few months, she would indeed enter Carmel. The book also recounts her spiritual growth in childhood and Carmel. Her first mention of the Sacred Heart devotion comes during her description of the Rome pilgrimage. The family stopped in Paris before going to Rome, and it was in Paris that the Martins made a solemn consecration to the Sacred Heart of Jesus at the Basilica of Montmartre.

While her autobiography is by far her most famous work, Therese was prolific. She wrote many letters to family and friends, and composed prayers and poetry. Taken as a whole, her work is a remarkable synthesis of Carmelite spirituality and the Sacred Heart devotion. Like other devotees of the Heart of Jesus, her writings are full of scriptural quotations and allusions, with the Gospel being her favorite source of inspiration. As a devout Carmelite, she often drew on the works of Saint Teresa of Avila and Saint John of the Cross. However, we also find mentions of the writings of Saint Gertrude and Saint Margaret Mary. Therese drew on all these rich sources as she developed a startling confidence in God based on being as a little child in her relationship with Him.

Growing up in a Catholic family in the France of her day, Therese would have been exposed to the Sacred Heart devotion as a matter of course. She had already integrated the devotion into her life by the age of ten. At that time she gave one of her sisters a birthday present consisting of a painting she had created of the Sacred Heart, surrounded by the famous words of Jesus to Saint Margaret Mary: "Behold this Heart which has so loved men."

Less than a month later, on Pentecost Sunday of 1883, Therese received an extraordinary grace and physical healing while looking at a statue of Mary in her home. At that time she saw the statue in a different way, because it appeared that Mary herself was present with a beautiful countenance and a warm smile for Therese. The child was immediately healed of a serious and seemingly intractable illness that had been plaguing her.

Therese was a touchy, hypersensitive child. Easily upset, she often burst into tears at the smallest perceived slight. Often she then became upset at having become upset, which simply prolonged her misery. At the age of thirteen, in 1886, Therese went to Midnight Christmas Mass and received Communion. Shortly after coming home that night, she met a situation that upset her but then received an extraordinary grace, which she described as the grace of complete conversion. She recovered her composure almost immediately and was freed from the hypersensitivity that had tormented and overwhelmed her all her life. While she remained extraordinarily sensitive, she received the strength to control her feelings and keep her emotional balance, even when she felt upset. A part of that grace was the ability to see that temporary problems—and all problems on earth are temporary—are often not worth getting upset about.

During the following year she felt increasingly called to pray for others, especially sinners. In July of 1887 Therese became aware of the trial and scheduled execution of Henri Pranzini, who had been convicted of murder in Paris. She was later to write that "everything pointed to the fact that he would die impenitent." Therese began praying and offering sacrifices for the man. Pranzini was executed on August 31 of that year. He was indeed impenitent until moments before his death, when he suddenly turned and took a crucifix a priest offered him. He kissed the crucifix three times. Therese read a newspaper account of the execution and interpreted the incident as a certain confirmation of her call to intercede for others.

Therese entered Carmel on April 9, 1888, at the age of fifteen. Her letters and other writings are sprinkled with references to the Sacred Heart of Jesus, but many mention this as a matter of course in passing. Occasionally, we catch a glimpse of how the devotion shaped her thinking and her relationship with Jesus. For example, in a letter to her sister Celine in 1889, she wrote, "The canticle of suffering united to His sufferings is what delights His Heart the most!"

France was still suffering the effects of Jansenism during this era. This was a school of thought (condemned by the Church) that put excessive emphasis on humanity's sinful nature and God's justice. Jansenists discouraged frequent reception of Communion because they charged that it would offend God. Therese, with her radical trust in God's merciful love, took a different view from the Jansenists, whose thinking still influenced many in France. An example is found in a letter from Therese to her beloved cousin, Marie Guerin, in which Therese corrects her cousin for failing to receive Communion on the Feast of the Ascension. Marie, beset by scruples, had decided against receiving Communion, believing it would have been a sacrilegious act. Therese had suffered from scruples for a time and shared her experiences with her cousin. "No, it is IMPOSSIBLE that a heart 'which rests only at the sight of the Tabernacle' offend Jesus to the point of not being able to receive Him; what offends Him and what wounds His Heart is the lack of confidence!"

Therese made her profession on September 8, 1890. During the following month, many people observed the second centenary of Margaret Mary Alacoque's death on October 17, 1690. Therese's sisters, Celine and Leonie Martin, planned to make a trip to the Visitation monastery in Paray for the occasion. A letter Therese wrote to Celine a few days before the trip provides more insights into how Therese formed a deeply intimate relationship with Jesus.

> Pray to the Sacred Heart; you know that I myself do not see the Sacred Heart as everybody else. I think that the Heart of my Spouse is mine alone, just as mine is His alone, and I speak to Him then in the solitude of this delightful heart to heart, while waiting to contemplate Him one day face to face...
>
> Do not forget your Therese over there; whisper only her name, and Jesus will understand. So many graces are attached there, especially for a soul that is suffering.

In another letter written to Celine later that month, Therese expressed complete confidence in the transforming power of the Heart of Jesus. "Celine, it seems to me that God has no need of *years* to carry out His work of love in a soul, a ray from His Heart can in one instant make His flower bloom for eternity!"

In 1893 Therese was explicitly synthesizing Carmelite spirituality and the Sacred Heart devotion. In a letter to her sister, Therese spoke of the ease with which people can grow closer to Jesus. "Oh, Celine how easy it is to please Jesus, to delight His Heart, one has only to love Him, without looking at one's self, without examining one's faults too much. Your Therese is not in the heights at this moment, but Jesus is teaching her to learn 'to draw profit from everything, *from the good* and *the bad* she finds in herself.'" In this passage Therese is quoting from Saint John of the Cross.

From 1893 on, Therese mentioned the Heart of Jesus more often in her writings. This was also the year when she began to write poetry. Some of the poems would mention, or be dedicated to, the Sacred Heart.

In 1894 Louis Martin, her beloved father, died after a lengthy illness, including dementia, and it was a trial for the entire family. Celine, who had long delayed her entrance into Carmel to care for her father, entered the Lisieux monastery.

By 1895 Therese had become even more prolific. She started work on her autobiography at the bidding of her sister and wrote many letters. She also composed prayers and poetry. In her autobiography she recounted an extraordinary grace she had received, which led to her making an offering of herself to God.

> This year, June 9, the Feast of the Holy Trinity, I received the grace to understand more than ever before how much Jesus desires to be loved.
>
> I was thinking about the souls who offer themselves as victims of God's Justice in order to turn away the punishments reserved to sinners, drawing them upon themselves. This offering seemed great and very generous to me, but I was far from feeling attracted to making it. From the depths of my heart, I cried out:
>
> "O my God! Will your Justice alone find souls willing to immolate themselves as victims? Does not Your *Merciful Love* need them too? On every side this love is unknown, rejected; those hearts upon whom you would lavish it turn to creatures, seeking happiness from them with their miserable affection; they do this instead

of throwing themselves into Your arms and of accepting Your infinite *Love*. O my God! Is your disdained Love going to remain closed up within Your Heart? It seems to me that if You were to find souls offering themselves as victims of holocaust to Your Love, You would consume them rapidly; it seems to me, too, that You would be happy not to hold back the waves of infinite tenderness within You. If Your Justice loves to release itself, this Justice *which extends only over the earth*, how much more does Your Merciful Love desire to *set souls on fire* since Your Mercy *reaches to the heavens*. O my Jesus, let me be this happy victim; consume Your holocaust with the fire of Your Divine Love!"

On this day Therese composed her famous Act of Oblation to Merciful Love, in which she offers herself as a holocaust. The Oblation contains several references to the Heart of Jesus, including this paragraph:

"After earth's Exile, I hope to go and enjoy you in the Fatherland, but I do not want to lay up merits for heaven. I want to work for Your *Love alone* with the one purpose of pleasing You, consoling

Your Sacred Heart, and saving souls who will love you eternally."

Various prayers, letters and poems Therese wrote that year refer to the Sacred Heart, and one poem is dedicated to His Heart. However, Therese draws on a passage in the Gospel that is not usually directly associated with the Heart of Jesus as her source of inspiration.

To the Sacred Heart of Jesus

At the holy sepulcher, Mary Magdelene,
Searching for her Jesus, stooped down in tears.
The angels wanted to console her sorrow,
But nothing could calm her grief.
Bright angels, it was not you
Whom this fervent soul came searching for.
She wanted to see the Lord of the Angels,
To take him in her arms, to carry him far away.

Close by the tomb, the last one to stay,
She had come well before dawn.
Her God also came, veiling his light.
Mary could not vanquish him in love!
Showing her at first his Blessed Face,
Soon just one word sprang from his Heart.
Whispering the sweet name of: Mary,
Jesus gave back peace, her happiness.

O my God, one day, like Mary Magdalene,
I wanted to see you and come close to you.

I looked down over the immense plain
Where I sought the Master and King,
And I cried, seeing the pure wave,
The starry azure, the flower, and the bird:
"Bright nature, if I do not see God,
You are nothing to me but a vast tomb.

"I need a heart burning with tenderness,
Who will be my support forever,
Who loves everything in me, even my weakness…
And who never leaves me day and night."
I could find no creature
Who could always love me and never die.
I must have a God who takes on my nature
And becomes my brother and is able to suffer!

You heard me, only Friend whom I love.
To ravish my heart, you became man.
You shed your blood, what a supreme mystery!…
And you still live for me on the Altar.
If I cannot see the brilliance of your Face
Or hear your sweet voice,
O my God, I can live by your grace,
I can rest on your Sacred Heart!

O Heart of Jesus, treasure of tenderness,
You Yourself are my happiness, my only hope.
You who knew how to charm my tender youth,
Stay near me till the last night.
Lord, to you alone I've given my life,
And all my desires are well-known to you.

It's in your ever-infinite goodness
That I want to lose myself, O Heart of Jesus!

Ah! I know well, all our righteousness
Is worthless in your sight.
To give value to my sacrifices,
I want to cast them into your Divine Heart.
You did not find your angels without blemish.
In the midst of lightning you gave your law!…
I hide myself in your Sacred Heart, Jesus.
I do not fear, my virtue is You!…

To be able to gaze on your glory,
I know we have to pass through fire.
So I, for my purgatory,
Choose your burning love, O heart of my God!
On leaving this life, my exiled soul
Would like to make an act of pure love,
And then, flying away to Heaven, its Homeland,
Enter straightaway into your Heart.

In another poem, composed later that year, Therese began with an epigraph quoting some words of Jesus to Saint Gertrude. He urged Gertrude to write down and often reread words of His that most exude love. The epigraph ends with these words: "Be assured then that the most precious relics of mine on earth are my words of love, the words that have come from my most sweet Heart."

In 1896, which was to be her last full year on earth, Therese continued work on her autobiography and again wrote many letters and poems. On April 2, Holy Thursday night, she had her first incident of coughing up blood, a sign of the tuberculosis that would eventually take her life. Sometime on Easter Sunday or shortly after that, she plunged into a spiritual darkness that would persist until her death. She called this her trial of faith but revealed little about the experience. However, many have inferred that Therese underwent what Saint John of the Cross calls the "Night of Faith," an excruciating experience in which the Lord purifies His loved ones by removing all spiritual consolation and comfort for a time.

Therese wrote a poem about heaven on the Feast of the Sacred Heart of Jesus that year. But reading this poem and other writings from this final stage of her life, we find no hint of the spiritual darkness that enshrouded her soul.

During 1897, the last year of her life, we find Therese writing about the Sacred Heart in poetry, prayer and correspondence. By then some of her sisters were beginning to recognize what an extraordinary soul she was, and they also suspected that she would not be with them much longer. They began to write down some of the things she said. These writing have been consolidated in *St. Therese of Lisieux: Her Last Conversations*. Here we find mentions of Saint

Gertrude and Saint Margaret Mary, who helped to shape her devotion to the Sacred Heart. And Therese reported that she had experienced great pain in her side on the Feast of the Sacred Heart.

In a letter written that month, Therese said that she believed Saint Mary Magdalene was moved to repentance because "she understood the abysses of love and mercy *of the Heart of Jesus.*"

Therese then went on to describe how His Heart had shaped her own spirituality. "Ever since I have been given the grace to understand also the love of the Heart of Jesus, I admit that it has expelled all fear from my heart. The remembrance of my faults humbles me, draws me never to depend on my strength which is only weakness, but this remembrance speaks to me of mercy and love even more."

Saint Therese experienced extraordinary physical and spiritual suffering during her final months. On the evening of September 30, 1897, she entered into an agony. Her body rattled as she tried to breathe; her face turned blue, her hands purple.

As she gazed at her Crucifix, she said, "Oh, I love Him! My God...I love you!"

As her sisters knelt around her in prayer, Saint Therese entered a silent ecstasy. Her face regained its normal color, and one of her sisters later wrote that her eyes appeared "brilliant with peace and joy." Then she took her last breath.

Saint Therese had practiced the Sacred Heart devotion since childhood, and it became an integral part of her life, shaping her relationship with Jesus to such an extraordinary extent that we find it in her letters, prayers, poems and even on her lips. Her devotion to the Sacred Heart nurtured her "little way" of growing closer to Jesus, and it eventually made her one of the most influential saints in the history of the Church.

In 1898 the Lisieux Carmel received permission to print *Story of a Soul*. Within a few years it was being translated into various languages, and it wasn't long before people all over the world thrilled at the inspiring words of Saint Therese. In 1914 a young Chilean girl in Santiago took up the book, receiving it with great joy.

Five

Teresa of the Andes:
The Saint of Infinite Joy

With joy you will draw water from
the wells of salvation
And you will say in that day:
Give thanks to the Lord,
call upon his name;
make known his deeds among the
nations,
proclaim that his name is exalted.
Sing praises to the Lord, for he has
done gloriously;
let this be known in all the earth.
Shout, and sing for joy, O inhabitant
of Zion,
for great in your midst is the Holy
One of Israel.

Isaiah 12:3–6

My soul magnifies the Lord,
and my spirit rejoices in God my
Savior.
    Luke 1:46–47

If you keep my commandments,
you will abide in my love, just as I
have kept my Father's commandments and abide in his love. These
things I have spoken to you, that
my joy may be in you, and that your
joy may be full.
    John 15:10–11

Juana Fernandez Solar was born on July 13, 1900, in Santiago, Chile. She was baptized two days later. At the baptismal font she was given the name Juana Enriqueta Josefina of the Sacred Hearts of Jesus and Mary. To friends and family, she quickly became known as Juanita.

Juanita was the fourth of six children born into a wealthy, aristocratic family. While their primary home was in Santiago, the family owned and managed large tracts of farming and ranch land outside the city. Juanita's father was often absent for long periods of time to manage the business.

Juanita later said that in her early years she was timid and sensitive, and she cried easily when upset. She grew up in a devout Catholic family. Her preschool years were largely unremarkable, but at the age of six she started having a great desire to receive Communion during Mass. She asked her mother if she could, but was told she had to wait until she was older.

Meanwhile, her brother Luis introduced her to devotion to the Blessed Virgin Mary. He prayed the rosary with her every day, and they made a promise to each other to pray the rosary daily for the rest of their lives. She later said she kept this commitment except for only one day, when she forgot. It was at this time that Juanita started to change. She said she had previously been subject to "ferocious fits of anger" on rare occasions, but she was able to put these behind her, even resisting when her brothers or sisters would deliberately try to incite her.

Her parents enrolled her in a school the Religious of the Sacred Heart ran when she was seven years old. Juanita asked her mother almost every day for permission to receive Communion, but for years was told she had to wait until she was older. Finally she received permission, spent the better part of a year preparing for the occasion, and was able to make great progress during the month of June, as she recounted in her diary. "In the month of the Sacred Heart I modified my character completely. I did this to such an extent that my mother was happy to see me preparing myself so well for my First Communion."

During this month she learned to obey promptly. After more preparation she received

Jesus in the Eucharist for the first time on September 11, 1910.

"My First Communion was a cloudless day," she recounted. "It's impossible to describe what took place between my soul and Jesus. I asked Him a thousand times that He would take me, and I experienced His dear voice for the first time." And that experience would continue. "Every day I went to Communion and talked with Jesus for a long time."

Juanita believed that these intimate dialogues with Jesus were normal and assumed they were a universal experience. One day she happened to mention to her mother something Jesus had told her at Communion time. Her mother, startled, suggested she talk to the parish priest about her experience. After that Juanita became more reserved about what was going on in her soul.

The Blessed Virgin Mary also took an active role in Juanita's life, and sometimes Juanita had conversations with her as well. Mysteriously, Juanita experienced serious illnesses, some of which appeared life threatening, on the Feast of the Immaculate Conception for several consecutive years.

Her experience of illness was to be a turning point. One day during a mild illness, Jesus revealed Himself to her and called her into Carmel. Juanita and her sister were both sick, and for a time Juanita was left alone, while a servant went to care for her sister. Juanita, troubled and envious, began to cry. "My tearful eyes began to fix themselves on a picture of the Sacred Heart, and I heard a very sweet voice say to me: 'What! I, Juanita, am alone on the altar for your love, and you can't even suffer for a moment?' From that time, the dear Jesus spoke to me, and I spent entire hours conversing with Him." Jesus told her He wanted her to learn how to suffer bravely and that He desired intimate union with her. "Then He told me that He wanted me for Himself, that he would like me to become a Carmelite."

While Jesus was preparing Juanita for a brief but extraordinary life, few people except her mother would have guessed the Lord was working wonders in this young girl. Juanita was a diligent student at school but led a balanced life. One of her hallmarks was a great sense of humor. She enjoyed playing friendly practical jokes on others and seemed to enjoy it just as much when others played such tricks on her. Laughter was a regular part of her life, and on several occasions she recounted that she and her friends would burst into uncontrollable, infectious laughter about one funny incident or another. Juanita was also musically gifted and learned to play the piano and the harmonium, an instrument similar to the organ.

In a recollection of her life, her brother Luis recalled that she had the harmonium in her bedroom, which was next to his. "In the morning while everyone was asleep, she used to play it very quietly with the soft pedal on, and I can still hear those muffled notes coming toward me. Even after fifty years, I am still moved to hear them. I asked Juanita why she did that, and she answered with luminous simplicity: 'It's because when day breaks I like to greet God by singing.'"

Juanita was also a gifted athlete. She excelled at swimming and won competitions in some swim meets she participated in. She was an active tennis player and thoroughly enjoyed the game. Most of all, she loved horseback riding, which she had learned from her grandfather at his hacienda when she was very young. When on vacation she would go riding for hours at a stretch. Juanita was such a skilled and daring rider that her friends sometimes jokingly referred to her as an Amazon.

In 1914 Juanita read the autobiography of Therese of Lisieux, which had a great influence on her. She identified strongly with Therese, and her reading of the autobiography reinforced her desire to become a Carmelite. Mysteriously, she also had an intuition that she would die young, as Therese had.

When she was fifteen years old, Juanita's parents decided to put her in a boarding school run by the Religious of the Sacred Heart. Juanita struggled to adapt to the change because she was so close to her family. Ultimately, the move prepared her for her eventual departure for the Carmelite convent in Los Andes, north of Santiago.

One of Juanita's most remarkable characteristics was a deep happiness and ebullient joy that often infected those around her. In letters to friends, she simply exulted in the beauties of nature she encountered on vacations. She described states of ecstasy when receiving Communion or adoring Jesus in the Blessed Sacrament; however, her joy was often born of pain that wasn't obvious to her friends. Hers was the pain of dying to self and surrendering her will to God; it was the struggle to become obedient to God in all things—the pain of the cross.

In her diary she revealed that Jesus gave her this combination of pain and joy. "He told me that He joyfully ascended Calvary and laid His head on the cross for the salvation of humankind. 'Is it possible that you are the one searching for Me and you want to be like Me? Then, come with Me and take up the cross with love and joy.'"

The three pillars of Juanita's spirituality were devotion to the Sacred Heart of Jesus, an ardent love for Him in the Blessed Sacrament and a passionate determination to do God's will regardless of what it cost her. She looked for faults in herself to correct and tried to apply herself to growing in virtue through prayer and sacrifice. Because others perceived her as happy most of the time, her heroic efforts to correspond to the great graces she received were easily overlooked. On occasion she revealed the struggles she was having. For example, while on vacation she wrote a letter to a friend in which she expressed sentiments about school that many young students have had at one time or another. "Only seven days before we must be in that dungeon. My blood runs cold just thinking about it…I wish they'd burn the school down."

Just a month later, she wrote a lengthy letter to her sister Rebecca in which she revealed her vocation to Carmel. The two girls were close, and Juanita knew Rebecca would be upset at the thought of losing her sister to a cloistered monastery. Still, Juanita revealed herself as exultant at the thought of consecrating herself to God. "How happy I am, my dear sister! I've been captured in the loving nets of The Divine Fisherman."

One of Juanita's most delightful characteristics was her extraordinary capacity for, and appreciation of, intimate friendship. She was close to a group of girls her age. When separated, they stayed in touch by writing letters, and Juanita's letters effuse care for her friends. She could be chatty, describing outings with family or friends, encouraging those who were considering religious vocations, and she showed a genuine interest in her friends' activities, religious or otherwise. In one letter she showed the typical interest of a teenage girl in social activities. "Please tell me all the news, and also if you're going with boys and all your impressions, too, like you did last year and in your latest letter."

Shortly after that, she wrote a different kind of letter to Graciela Montes Larrain, a friend who was considering a religious vocation. In it Juanita revealed that she felt a strong attraction to Carmel and asked her friend for help in her spiritual growth. "Please help me become good. Tell me what you plan to do during the month of the Sacred Heart. Let's ask our dear Jesus what He desires of us. Let's consecrate ourselves to Him. Let's give Him our heart, our freedom, and all we have."

Juanita then went on to ask her friend for help in identifying any faults Juanita might have so she could work on changing them.

These letters of encouragement emerge as a subgenre in Juanita's writings and were to have a great influence on others. At least four of her close friends eventually joined religious orders (including Graciela, who became a Carmelite). Juanita's sister, Rebecca, was also to become a Carmelite sister, while her mother became a Third Order (lay) Carmelite.

Juanita's love for her friends led her to tailor her letters in an exquisite way. One letter might share her experience of Jesus in the Eucharist, while another, to someone who was less religious, mostly involved news of family and friends. And while she had a serious tone when writing about her relationship with God, she also sprinkled her letters with humorous remarks. At the end of one lengthy letter, she wrote, "I don't want to end this letter, but charity obliges me to do so, because I've been boring you long enough."

While Juanita's letters show great care and concern for her friends, she was balanced and knew how to receive love as well as give it, and she showed a deep appreciation for the gift of friendship, as in one letter, where she wrote, "I'm still savoring the conversation we had. I see how really valuable a good friend is. I truly understand the need of opening my heart to someone who understands me and feels the same as I do. How much good you've done for me. I thank you with my whole heart."

And in another letter, she wrote of hoping to spend more time with a close friend. "We will try to see each other more frequently, for I feel that friendship is a great help in keeping us on the path of perfection."

In her diary Juanita often wrote of the Sacred Heart of Jesus, both as a reference point and a living reality. For example, she wrote about an incident at school where she became childishly angry and later reflected on the experience. "Dear Jesus, what do you say about this soldier who is so cowardly and so imperfect? Forgive me. The next time I'll be better. I'll throw myself into that immense ocean of the love of your Heart, to lose myself in It like a drop of water in the ocean and to abase my littleness in the greatness of Your mercy."

During the following month, Juanita recounted an encounter with Jesus.

> Last night I spent one hour with Jesus. We were speaking intimately. He reproached me because in my pains and doubts I didn't have recourse to His Heart as I used to. He desires that I be a virgin, without being touched by any creatures, because I must belong entirely to Him. I rested myself on His Heart. Then he spoke to me about poverty. I came away from Him without a thing. Everything belongs to Him. Everything passes away and is vanity...He told me that I should suffer with joy and with love, and every day I should remove a thorn from His Heart.

As time went on, Juanita grew more concerned about renouncing her own will to become more like Jesus. To one friend she wrote, "Let's live on the cross. The cross is the abnegation of our will. Heaven is on the cross, because Jesus is there."

Juanita had read and reread Saint Therese's autobiography. In 1917 she expanded her reading to include other Carmelites. She read Saint Teresa of Avila's autobiography and works by Blessed Elizabeth of the Trinity. In September of 1917 she wrote to Mother Angelica Teresa, the prioress of the Carmelite monastery at Los Andes, for the first time. Juanita told of her interest in becoming a Carmelite and shared her concern about potential barriers, including poor health and possible opposition from her family. Mother Angelica responded warmly, and a lively correspondence followed. In later letters Juanita would share her hesitations about entering Carmel, because she thought of herself as having many faults. While she yearned to enter Carmel, she was honest about her faults. In any case she still needed to complete her formal schooling, and she was too young to enter Carmel right away.

Despite her strong attraction to Carmel, Juanita sometimes had serious doubts about her vocation. Schooled by the Religious of the Sacred Heart, she had come to admire their way of life, combining an active ministry with prayer, and she considered becoming a Sacred Heart sister. Juanita eventually consulted several priests to help her decide whether her Carmelite vocation was authentic.

In January of 1919 Juanita and her mother took a trip to the Los Andes Carmel. They went in secrecy, expecting opposition from other family members. They spent the afternoon there, and Juanita was able to go to the adjoining church when it was time for Vespers. The sisters recited the Divine Office with such devotion that Juanita was moved to tears of gratitude. During the visit Juanita experienced such deep feelings of peace and gratitude that her doubts about having a Carmelite vocation vanished. She had the opportunity to meet the whole community and was struck by how warm and loving the sisters were. The following day she wrote a letter of thanks to Mother Angelica in which she reported, "That one little visit to my convent filled my soul with joy."

Shortly after the visit, Juanita had her summer vacation from school, which she spent on a farm owned by a friend's family. During that time some priests came to give a mission to the local residents. Juanita and some other girls took the opportunity to hold catechism classes for the young children of the area, which they continued for a time even after the mission was complete. Juanita reported in a letter to a friend that about fifty children came to the classes, which were well received. "The people here know very little. It seems that they're being taught little or nothing at the public school." Every day the girls traveled by horseback to consecrate homes to the Sacred Heart of Jesus.

Meanwhile, Juanita had yet to broach the question of entering Carmel with her father. She chose the Feast of the Annunciation to write him a long letter, explaining her vocation and asking his permission to go. Juanita described how she had developed a great love for Mary when she was young and said the Blessed Virgin Mary "placed the seed of a vocation in my soul." Then she went on to describe other developments, including a flirtation with a boy. "But when I came down with a case of appendicitis and saw myself very sick, I began thinking about what life was all about; and one day when I was alone in my room, weary of staying in bed, I heard the voice of the Sacred Heart asking me if I belonged entirely to Him. I don't think it was an illusion, because at that instant I saw myself transformed. Till then I had been searching for the love of creatures, and now I desired God alone."

She went on to describe Carmel in glowing terms and begged her father for permission to enter the convent in May. While she wrote persuasively—he did give his permission despite many qualms—Juanita at that time was enduring a terrible period of spiritual darkness, the kind God often uses to purify souls. The next day she wrote to a priest, describing her interior life.

"I experience only horrible dryness in my prayer. It's of such a nature that I find myself immersed in darkness, and it's impossible for me to keep my thoughts on God nor can I recollect myself. When I go to Communion, I don't feel a thing. I'm like a stone with our Lord; so much so, Rev. Father, that desires come to me of not wanting to receive Communion because of the evil I do."

Juanita received her father's permission to enter Carmel, but her decision caused enormous upheaval in her family; her brother Luis and others bitterly opposed her choice and made every effort to dissuade her. Various family members burst into tears during some of these discussions, but Juanita remained peaceful and steadfast during the conversations. When she was alone again in her room, however, she would weep because, as much as she wanted to enter Carmel, the thought of being separated from her beloved family caused her much pain.

Juanita finally fulfilled her dream of entering Carmel on May 7, 1919. Her name in religion was Teresa of Jesus, in honor of the great Saint Teresa of Avila. Normally, postulants in Carmel aren't given permission to write many letters to those outside the monastery. Providentially, the superior gave Sister Teresa permissions far beyond the norm in this area. The result is an extraordinary record of her growing love for God and her transformation in Him. The content of her letters changed as soon as she entered Carmel. She wrote almost exclusively of God and life in Carmel, rarely touching on other topics, although she remained sweetly thoughtful, always concerned about how her family and friends were doing.

Sister Teresa's first letter, written the day after she entered Carmel, was to her father. She thanked him yet again for giving her permission to enter the convent and reported on how she was doing. "You can't imagine how happy I am being here. I've found heaven on earth at last. Although it's true that yesterday I left my family with my heart in tatters, today I enjoy unalterable peace."

Just a few days later, she wrote a similar letter to her brother Luis. "Oh! If only for a moment you could feel yourself filled with the happiness I feel. Believe me, at every moment I ask myself whether I'm in heaven, since I find myself wrapped in a divine atmosphere of peace, love, light and infinite joy."

Sister Teresa felt that the other sisters loved and cared for her. While she enjoyed the solitude of her cell, she also appreciated the music and camaraderie of the community recreation periods, which she described as full of joking and laughter. Besides getting on well with the other sisters, she even managed to win the affection of a dog who lived on the grounds. Molzuc, the dog, had a reputation for being fierce with strangers and newcomers to the community, but he took a liking to Sister Teresa immediately, prompting one of the other sisters to remark, "Look. Even the dogs love her."

Only a week after entering Carmel, Sister Teresa wrote a letter to a friend, in which she described the Carmelite vocation as one of being an adoring victim, where a sister tried to fulfill God's will at every moment of the day. She described the intensive efforts one must make to practice renunciation of self-will and live simply. "Let's humble ourselves, seeing our lowliness, and let's raise our spirit to God. May we always live joyfully. God is infinite joy."

During the month of June Teresa was edified by how the community observed the month of the Sacred Heart with such recollection and devotion. Her passionate love for God seemed to reach new heights of fervor. She wrote to family members and friends describing how happy she was to be able to focus her attention on Jesus, as in a letter to her brother Luis "When people love, they can't help speaking of their loved one. What happens then if the one loved has within Himself every possible perfection? I don't know how I can do a thing but contemplate and love Him. What can you expect, if Jesus Christ, that Mad Lover, has made me fall madly in love with Himself?"

In a similar vein she wrote to a friend, "I'm the happiest person alive. I lack for nothing because my whole being is satiated with the love of God… This Friday ask the Sacred Heart of Jesus to make you love Him and be His friend. What a treasury you'll find in that Divine Heart! Day and night He's knocking at your heart's door, asking you for a little spot there, for a little love. Won't you open up to Him, offering Him your warmth? He's calling out to you from the tabernacle. From out of eternity, He's been wanting you to receive Him in Communion every day."

In subsequent months Sister Teresa's fervent love for Jesus in the Blessed Sacrament became more ardent. She would frequently describe Communion as a moment of heaven, a time of exquisite intimacy with the Lord. "If we prepared ourselves every morning a little better to receive Communion, how much we'd draw from our Communion, how we would spend the entire day in an ecstasy of love with that immense, majestic God become food for our souls!"

Eventually, the presence of God came to permeate Sister Teresa's life in an extraordinary way, whether she was in the chapel or elsewhere.

I rejoice to the intimate depths of my being to see Him so beautiful, to experience that I'm always united with Him, for God is immense and present everywhere...If you give yourself to prayer, you'll find that God will show Himself to you, and make you fall in love with Him. In prayer our soul seeks Him out, and if we do so, wanting to know and love Him, Jesus will raise the veil that conceals Him and show us His divine Face, radiant with beauty and sweetness. There are times when He will open His Heart's wound, and will show us the treasures of his infinite goodness and love. At other

times, He lets His sweet voice be
heard, leaving the soul consumed
by love and repentance.

Saint Teresa's increasingly intimate relationship with Jesus fueled her ardor. While she, like
many Christians, sometimes had painful periods
of spiritual aridity, her passionate love enabled
her to experience the vibrant, living reality of
Jesus in the Eucharist. She begged other people to accompany her, as in this letter to a friend.
"Try every morning, when you have the joy of
receiving Communion, to ask our Lord to remain
with you all day in your soul…When I think now
of how I used to be envious of Mary Magdalene
for having had Jesus in her home so often, for
having heard Him, I'm ashamed, since He has
not abandoned this world. He's present in the
Tabernacle. I gaze upon Him in faith, and hear
Him."

In September of 1919 Sister Teresa made a
retreat. We find in her diary resolutions she made
to live out her vocation.

> The Carmelite must ascend the
> Tabor of Carmel and be clothed
> with the garments of penance that
> will make her more like Jesus. And,
> as He, she wants to be transformed,
> to be transfigured in order to be
> converted into God.

The Carmelite must ascend Calvary. There she will immolate herself for souls. Love crucifies her; she dies to herself and to the world. She is buried, and her tomb is the Heart of Jesus; and from there she rises, is reborn to a new life and spiritually lives united to the whole world.

Teresa saw that the same graces of sanctification available to vowed religious are available to laypeople as well, as she explained in a letter written in November of 1919. "For a Carmelite, Communion is heaven; and Communion should be the same for every believing soul. Why don't we die of love in seeing that God found it far too little to give us His infinite love drop by drop? In his infinite love He wants to give us more, and yet humanity prepares His death. He becomes our food in order to give us life. A God who is nourishment, bread for His creatures; isn't that enough to make us die of love?"

In retrospect her letter was clearly prophetic. Sometime in March of 1920, Sister Teresa told her confessor that God had given her the understanding that she would die within a month. By Holy Week she was ill, but she spent hours before the Blessed Sacrament. On Good Friday, April 2, the novice mistress noticed that Teresa's cheeks were very red and discovered she had a raging fever. Sister Teresa suffered terribly the following day. She had typhus, and several doctors treated her, but the illness continued. Sister Teresa was able to receive Communion several times during the following days.

Typhus can cause delirium, and Teresa suffered in a delirious state during parts of her illness; however, she had periods of clarity. She hadn't made her religious vows because she was still a novice, but she received permission to make her profession due to the imminent danger of death. Sister Teresa pronounced her vows as a Carmelite on April 7 and also received Communion for the last time. She died on April 12.

Saint Teresa of the Andes had been in Carmel only eleven months at the time of her death. She was nineteen years old.

At her funeral on April 14, her community was astonished at the throngs who flocked to the Mass, including many people who had never met Saint Teresa. By word of mouth in the region, people had learned that an extraordinarily holy sister had died. Her brother Luis noticed people pointing in his direction, whispering that he was the brother of the saint.

Today, in an era when so many people experience sadness and loneliness, Saint Teresa of the Andes offers a model of genuine joy and authentic, intimate friendships.

Pope John Paul II beatified Teresa in Santiago in 1987. During his homily John Paul said that the secret of Teresa's perfection was her love for Jesus and her love for Mary. "For her, God is infinite joy. This is the new hymn of Christian love that rises spontaneously from the soul of this young Chilean girl, in whose glorified face we can sense the grace of her transformation in Christ. She possessed an understanding, serving, humble and patient love, a love which does not destroy human values, but rather elevates and transfigures them."

Pope John Paul II canonized Saint Teresa of the Andes in Rome in 1993. In his homily he noted that she had adopted and lived the motto of the great Saint Teresa of Avila, founder of the Discalced Carmelites. And he went on to recommend Saint Teresa of the Andes as a model and intercessor for young people.

> The life of Blessed Teresa cries out continually from within her cloister, "God alone suffices."
> She shouts it out particularly to the young people who hunger for the truth and seek a light which will give direction to their lives. To young people who are being allured by the continuous messages and stimuli of an erotic culture, a society which mistakes the hedonistic exploitation of another for genuine

love, which is self-giving, this young virgin of the Andes today proclaims the beauty and happiness that comes from a pure heart.

Six

Divine Mercy

Those who trust in him will understand truth,
and the faithful will abide with him
in love,
because grace and mercy are upon
his elect,
and he watches over his holy ones.
    Wisdom of Solomon 3:9

Have mercy on me, O God, according to thy steadfast love;
according to thy abundant mercy
blot out my transgressions.
    Psalm 51:1

Jesus looked up and said to her,
"Woman, where are they? Has no
one condemned you?" She said,
"No one, Lord." And Jesus said,

> "Neither do I condemn you; go,
> and do not sin again."
> John 8:10–11

The Heart of Jesus was pierced for love of us on Calvary, and the blessings of His merciful love have been poured out on humanity in an extraordinary stream of grace ever since. Yet in the twentieth century, Jesus gave a Polish nun a revelation of His Heart that emphasized a simply astonishing mercy that would cleanse all who approached Him with trust. The message of mercy, so intimately intertwined with the devotion to the Sacred Heart, spread rapidly. The Divine Mercy image can now be found in churches and homes all over the world. Millions of people have learned to pray the Chaplet of Divine Mercy, a beautiful prayer that draws down the blessing of the Father of mercies in torrents of grace that convert sinners and save many souls from damnation. The universal Church, in response to a request Jesus made, now observes the Sunday after Easter as a special Feast of Mercy. This devotion prepares the world for the Second Coming of Christ.

The story of this devotion and of the woman who would become the Apostle of Divine Mercy begins in the heart of Poland. Helen Kowalska was born to a farming family in the village of Glogowiec, near Lodz, on August 25, 1905. She was the third of ten children. Helen was attracted to the grace of God even in childhood and would sometimes rise in the middle of the night to pray.

The upheaval in Europe and the ensuing First World War had a profound effect on Poland during Helen's childhood, and many schools were closed during that period. When they reopened, some students were given only a few years of education before they were pushed out to make room for younger students. As a result Helen received only two years of formal education. As a teenager she worked as a housekeeper for a time. God spoke to her in her heart, calling her to the religious life. Through a series of locutions, God guided her to a convent of the Congregation of the Sisters of Our Lady of Mercy in Warsaw, which Helen entered on August 1, 1925.

The sisters of the order worked with troubled girls and young women, including prostitutes, by giving them a safe place to stay, education and spiritual formation. Within a few weeks, Helen was severely tempted to leave the convent, because the life there was so active, and she thought she would be better suited to a more contemplative order. However, Jesus Himself appeared to her to tell her to remain in that order. "It is to this place that I called you and nowhere else; and I have prepared many graces for you."

After spending some time in that convent, she was transferred to a much larger one in the Lagiewniki neighborhood in Cracow. It would be the first of many moves from one convent to another that she would make, and it was here that she would take the habit and veil and serve her novitiate for two years. On April 30, 1926, Helen received the habit and her religious name: Sister Mary Faustina.

During the novitiate she had a dream in which she encountered the saint of radical trust, as she recounted in her diary.

> I want to write down a dream that I had about Saint Therese of the Child Jesus. I was still a novice at the time and was going through some difficulties I did not know how to overcome. They were interior difficulties connected with exterior ones. I made novenas to various saints, but the situation grew worse and more difficult. The sufferings it caused me were so great that I did not know how to go on living, but suddenly the thought occurred to me that I should pray to Saint Therese of the Child Jesus. I started a novena to this Saint, because before entering the convent I had had a great devotion to her. Lately I had somewhat neglected this devotion, but in my need I began again to pray with great fervor.

On the fifth day of the novena, I dreamed of Saint Therese, but it was as if she were still living on earth. She hid from me the fact that she was a saint and began to comfort me, saying that I should not be worried about this matter, but should trust more in God. She said, "I suffered greatly, too," but I did not quite believe her and said, "It seems to me that you have not suffered at all." But Saint Therese answered me in a convincing manner that she had suffered very much indeed and said to me, "Sister, know that in three days the difficulty will come to a happy conclusion." When I was not very willing to believe her, she revealed to me that she was a saint. At that moment, a great joy filled my soul, and I said to her, "You are a saint?" "Yes," she answered, "I am a saint. Trust that this matter will be resolved in three days." And I said, "Dear sweet Therese, tell me, shall I go to heaven?" And she answered, "Yes, you will go to heaven, Sister." "And will I be a saint?" To which she replied, "Yes, you will be a saint." "But, little Therese, shall I be a saint as you are, raised to the altar?" And

she answered, "Yes, you will be a
saint just like I am, but you must
trust in the Lord Jesus."

In her diary she went on to describe how she
questioned the saint about the spiritual well-being
of her parents and siblings, then summed up her
view of the experience. "This was a dream. And
as the proverb goes, dreams are phantoms; God
is faith. Nevertheless, three days later the difficulty was solved very easily, just as she had said.
And everything in this affair turned out exactly as
she said it would. It was a dream, but it had its
significance."

After Sister Faustina made temporary vows,
she was moved several times. The extraordinary
revelations she would receive began even before
she made her final profession. In her diary she
gave an account of the events of February 22,
1931.

In the evening, when I was in my
cell, I saw the Lord Jesus clothed in
a white garment. One hand [was]
raised in the gesture of blessing,
the other was touching the garment at the breast. From beneath
the garment, slightly drawn aside
at the breast, there were emanating
two large rays, one red, the other
pale. In silence I kept my gaze fixed

on the Lord; my soul was struck with awe, but also with great joy. After a while, Jesus said to me, "Paint an image according to the pattern you see, with the signature: Jesus, I trust in You. I desire that this image be venerated, first in your chapel, and [then] throughout the world.

"I promise that the soul that will venerate this image will not perish. I also promise victory over [its] enemies already here on earth, especially at the hour of death. I Myself will defend it as My own glory."

Sister Faustina told her confessor about this vision, and he told her it meant she was to paint God's image in her soul. She continued her account in her diary.

When I came out of the confessional, I again heard words such as these: "My image already is in your soul. I desire that there be a Feast of Mercy. I want this image, which you will paint with a brush, to be solemnly blessed on the first Sunday after Easter; that Sunday is to be the Feast of Mercy.

"I desire that priests proclaim this great mercy of Mine towards souls of sinners. Let the sinner not be afraid to approach Me. The flames of mercy are burning Me—clamoring to be spent; I want to pour them out upon these souls."

Jesus complained to me in these words, "Distrust on the part of souls is tearing at My insides. The distrust of a chosen soul causes Me even greater pain; despite My inexhaustible love for them they do not trust Me. Even My death is not enough for them. Woe to the soul that abuses these [gifts]."

While God was laying the groundwork for the Divine Mercy image and the celebration of Divine Mercy Sunday, he also gave Saint Faustina certain specific prayers to pray. One of the greatest is a short prayer for sinners that bathes them in mercy. She recounted the words of Jesus in her diary.

I desire that you know more profoundly the love that burns in My Heart for souls, and you will understand this when you meditate upon My Passion. Call upon My mercy on behalf of sinners; I desire their salvation. When you say this prayer, with a contrite heart and with faith on behalf of some sinner, I will give him the grace of conversion. This is the prayer:

O Blood and Water, which gushed forth from the Heart of Jesus as a fount of Mercy for us, I trust in You.

Sister Faustina made her perpetual vows on May 1, 1933. A few weeks later, she was transferred to her congregation's house in Vilnius.

Here we find her desire for God and her fervent faith enkindled by the Holy Spirit as she strove to love God in a totally unprecedented way. She wrote,

> I want to love You as no human soul has ever loved you before; and although I am utterly miserable and small, I have nevertheless cast the anchor of my trust deep down into the abyss of Your mercy, O my God and Creator! In spite of my great misery I fear nothing, but hope to sing you a hymn of glory for ever. Let no soul, even the most miserable, fall prey to doubt; for, as long as one is alive, each one can become a great saint, so great is the power of God's grace. It remains only for us not to oppose God's action.

139

In Vilnius Father Michael Sopocko became Sister Faustina's confessor and spiritual director, and he would play a significant role in the development and spread of the Divine Mercy message. While it had been some time since Jesus revealed Himself to Sister Faustina and requested that a painting of the image be created, very little progress had been made. Sister Faustina didn't know how to paint, and she had asked several sisters for help, but the results were totally unsatisfactory.

In 1934 Father Sopocko directed Sister Faustina to ask Jesus about the meaning of the two rays in the image. She recorded what Jesus told her.

> The two rays denote Blood and Water. The pale ray stands for the Water which makes souls righteous. The red ray stands for the Blood which is the life of souls.
>
> These two rays issued forth from the very depths of My tender mercy when my agonized Heart was opened by a lance on the Cross.
>
> These rays shield souls from the wrath of My Father. Happy is the one who will dwell in their shelter, for the just hand of God shall not lay hold of him. I desire that the first Sunday after Easter be the Feast of Mercy.

Ask of my faithful servant [Father Sopocko] that, on this day, he tell the whole world of My great mercy; that whoever approaches the Fount of Life on this day will be granted complete remission of sins and punishment.

Mankind will not have peace until it turns with trust to My mercy.

Oh, how much I am hurt by a soul's distrust! Such a soul professes that I am Holy and Just, but does not believe that I am Mercy and does not trust in My Goodness. Even the devils glorify My Justice but do not believe in My Goodness.

My Heart rejoices in this title of Mercy.

Proclaim that mercy is the greatest attribute of God. All the works of My hands are crowned with mercy.

Eventually Father Sopocko arranged to have Sister Faustina work closely with a professional artist, Eugene Kazimierowski, who would paint the first Divine Mercy image, using her description of her vision of Jesus as a basis for his work. She met with the artist regularly as the work proceeded. After one such visit she came away feeling sad because the painting, of course, could not capture the infinite splendor and majesty of

Jesus. She recounted that she returned to the chapel in her convent and wept a great deal, asking the Lord, "Who will paint You as beautiful as You are?"

"Not in the beauty of the color, nor of the brush lies the greatness of this image, but in My grace," Jesus said.

On another occasion, Jesus told her, "My gaze from this image is like My gaze from the cross."

Father Sopocko also directed her to ask the Lord about where the words should appear on the image, because as the work proceeded, there didn't seem to be room enough for everything. Jesus reminded her of what He had first told her, that the words "Jesus, I trust in You" ("Jezu, Ufam Tobie" in Polish) were to be an integral part of the image. The signature words express a commitment to firm trust in Jesus.

"I am offering people a vessel with which they are to keep coming for graces to the fountain of mercy. That vessel is this image with the signature: 'Jesus, I trust in You.'"

The image was completed in 1934. Since then other artists have used Sister Faustina's description as a basis for different versions of the image, and God has poured out His blessings on humanity through these images, confirming that the greatness of the image lies in His grace. The original image was first placed in a convent and would be displayed publicly in a church for the first time in 1935.

While Jesus made use of the image to enrich His people, He still emphasized His presence in the Eucharist as a radiant source of infinite blessings. However, he also lamented to Sister Faustina that people didn't always accept his graces.

> My Heart overflows with great mercy for souls, and especially for poor sinners. If only they could understand that I am the best of Fathers to them and that it is for them that the Blood and Water flowed from My Heart as from a fount overflowing with mercy. For them I dwell in the tabernacle as King of Mercy. I desire to bestow My graces upon souls, but they do not want to accept them. You, at least, come to Me as often as possible and take these graces they do not want to accept. In this way you will console My Heart. Oh, how indifferent are souls to so much goodness, to so many proofs of love! My Heart drinks only of the ingratitude and forgetfulness of souls living in the world. They have time for everything, but they have no time to come to Me for graces.
> So I turn to you, you—chosen souls, will you also fail to understand

the love of My Heart? So many reservations, so much distrust, so much caution. To comfort you, let Me tell you that there are souls living in the world who love Me dearly. I dwell in their hearts with delight. But they are few. In convents, too, there are souls that fill My Heart with joy. They bear My features; therefore the Heavenly Father looks upon them with special pleasure. They will be a marvel to Angels and men. Their number is very small. They are a defense for the world before the justice of the Heavenly Father and a means of obtaining mercy for the world. The love and sacrifice of these souls sustain the world in existence. The infidelity of a soul specially chosen by Me wounds My Heart most painfully. Such infidelities are swords which pierce My Heart.

In His conversations with Sister Faustina, Jesus repeatedly returned to the themes of radical trust and incomprehensible mercy. On one occasion, as she was at adoration, He spoke to her again.

With souls that have recourse to My mercy and with those that glorify and proclaim My great mercy to others, I will deal according to My infinite mercy at the hour of their death.

My Heart is sorrowful because even chosen souls do not understand the greatness of My mercy. Their relationship [with Me] is, in certain ways, imbued with mistrust. Oh, how much that wounds My Heart! Remember My Passion, and if you do not believe My words, at least believe My wounds.

Jesus also told Saint Faustina about the transforming power of obedience in the life of souls. "Yes, when you are obedient I take away your weakness and replace it with My strength. I am very surprised that souls do not want to make that exchange with Me."

Meanwhile, Jesus continued to affirm His desire that the Sunday after Easter be set aside as a special Feast of Divine Mercy. In 1935 Sister Faustina attended a special celebration of the Jubilee of the Redemption that coincided with the Sunday after Easter. She described a vision she had experienced on that occasion.

Toward the end of the service, when the priest took the Blessed Sacrament to bless the people, I saw the Lord Jesus as He is represented in the image. The Lord gave

145

His blessing, and the rays extended over the whole world. Suddenly, I saw an impenetrable brightness in the form of a crystal dwelling place, woven together from waves of a brilliance unapproachable to both creatures and spirits. Three doors led to this resplendence. At that moment, Jesus, as He is represented in the image, entered this resplendence through the second door to the Unity within. It is a triple Unity, which is incomprehensible—which is infinity. I heard a voice, "This Feast emerged from the very depths of My mercy, and it is confirmed in the vast depths of My tender mercies. Every soul believing and trusting in My mercy will obtain it."

During the following month, Jesus revealed to Sister Faustina that part of her mission was linked to His return. "You will prepare the world for My final coming," He said.

This was to be one of several times when He talked to Sister Faustina about His plans for the future. On another occasion He gave the following description:

Write this: before I come as the just Judge, I am coming first as the

King of Mercy. Before the day of justice arrives, there will be given to people a sign in the heavens of this sort:

All light in the heavens will be extinguished, and there will be great darkness over the whole earth. Then the sign of the cross will be seen in the sky, and from the openings where the hands and the feet of the Savior were nailed will come forth great lights which will light up the earth for a period of time. This will take place shortly before the last day.

While Sister Faustina often heard God's voice in her heart, she was also blessed with visions of the Blessed Virgin Mary from time to time. One year on the Feast of the Annunciation, while Sister Faustina was having her meditation, Mary appeared to her and spoke to her about the return of Jesus.

Oh, how pleasing to God is the soul that follows faithfully the inspirations of His grace! I gave the Savior to the world; as for you, you have to speak to the world about His great mercy and prepare the world for the Second Coming of

Him who will come, not as a merciful Savior, but as a just Judge. Oh, how terrible is that day! Determined is the day of justice, the day of divine wrath. The angels tremble before it. Speak to souls about this great mercy while it is still the time for [granting] mercy. If you keep silent now, you will be answering for a great number of souls on that terrible day. Fear nothing. Be faithful to the end. I sympathize with you.

Later Jesus taught Sister Faustina a prayer now known as the Chaplet of Divine Mercy. One day, as she was in prayer, He told her that the chaplet would help many to prepare for His coming. "Oh, what great graces I will grant to souls who say this chaplet; the very depths of My tender mercy are stirred for the sake of those who say the chaplet. Write down these words, My daughter. Speak to the world about My mercy; let all mankind recognize My unfathomable mercy. It is a sign for the end times; after it will come the day of justice. While there is still time, let them have recourse to the fount of My mercy; let them profit from the Blood and Water which gushed forth for them."

Jesus told Sister Faustina that both chaplet and Divine Mercy Sunday were being granted to the world to help prepare people for His return.

"Souls perish in spite of My bitter Passion. I am giving them the last hope of salvation; that is, the Feast of My Mercy. If they will not adore My mercy, they will perish for all eternity. Secretary of My mercy, write, tell souls about this great mercy of mine, because the awful day, the day of My justice, is near," He said.

Jesus began to teach Sister Faustina to pray the chaplet on Friday, September 13, 1935, as she recounted in her diary.

> In the evening, when I was in my cell, I saw an Angel, the executioner of divine wrath. He was clothed in a dazzling robe, his face gloriously bright, a cloud beneath his feet. From the cloud, bolts of thunder and flashes of lightning were springing into his hands; and from his hand they were going forth, and only then were they striking the earth. When I saw this sign of divine wrath which was about to strike the earth, and in particular a certain place, which for good reasons I cannot name, I began to implore the Angel to hold off for a few moments, and the world would do penance. But my plea was a mere nothing in the face of the divine anger. Just then I saw the Most Holy Trinity. The

greatness of Its majesty pierced me deeply, and I did not dare to repeat my entreaties. At that very moment I felt in my soul the power of Jesus' grace, which dwells in my soul. When I became conscious of this grace, I was instantly snatched up before the Throne of God. Oh, how great is our Lord and God and how incomprehensible His holiness! I will make no attempt to describe this greatness, because before long we shall all see Him as He is. I found myself pleading with God for the world with words heard interiorly.

As I was praying in this manner, I saw the Angel's helplessness; he could not carry out the just punishment which was rightly due for sins. Never before had I prayed with such inner power as I did then.

The words with which I entreated God were these: Eternal Father, I offer you the Body and Blood, Soul and Divinity of Your dearly beloved Son, Our Lord Jesus Christ for our sins and those of the whole world; for the sake of His sorrowful Passion, have mercy on us.

The next morning, when I entered chapel, I heard these words interiorly:

Every time you enter the chapel,
immediately recite the prayer which
I taught you yesterday. When I had
said the prayer, in my soul I heard
these words: This prayer will serve to
appease My wrath. You will recite it
for nine days, on the beads of the
rosary, in the following manner: First
of all, you will say one Our Father
and Hail Mary and the I Believe In
God. Then on the Our Father beads
you will say the following words:
"Eternal Father, I offer You the Body
and Blood, Soul and Divinity of Your
dearly beloved Son, Our Lord Jesus
Christ, in atonement for our sins and
those of the whole world." On the
Hail Mary beads you will say the following words: "For the sake of His
sorrowful Passion have mercy on us
and on the whole world." In conclusion, three times you will recite these
words: "Holy God, Holy Mighty One,
Holy Immortal One, have mercy on
us and on the whole world."

And so it was that God gave the world a
prayer that would convert sinners, obtain countless blessings from heaven, and even be powerful
enough to turn away divine wrath by appealing
to the very Heart of the Trinity.

In the very next entry in her diary, Sister Faustina wrote about silence, a topic she addressed repeatedly. Despite being in an active (as opposed to contemplative) religious congregation, she often wrote about silence as being an essential ingredient in the spiritual life.

"Silence is a sword in the spiritual struggle. A talkative soul will never attain sanctity. The sword of silence will cut off everything that would like to cling to the soul. We are sensitive to words and quickly want to answer back, without taking any regard as to whether it is God's will that we should speak. A silent soul is strong; no adversities will harm it if it perseveres in silence."

While she emphasized silence many time in her writing, she said she didn't mean an enforced, gloomy silence but an interior silence that enables one to be attentive to God and neighbor. "One can speak a great deal without breaking silence and, on the contrary, one can speak little and be constantly breaking silence," she noted.

Sister Faustina's love of silence grew out of her great love for Jesus and her desire to listen to Him. He taught her how to be attentive.

"I will tell you most when you converse with Me in the depths of your heart. Here, no one can disturb my actions. Here, I rest as in a garden enclosed," He said.

On another occasion Jesus told her about how important listening and reflection are.

"When you reflect upon what I tell you in the depths of your heart, you profit more than if you had read many books. Oh, if souls would only want to listen to My voice when I am speaking in the depths of their hearts, they would reach the peak of holiness in a short time," He said.

While Jesus said that people should live in a spirit of silence and recollection in order to hear His voice, He also told Sister Faustina that He desired true intimacy with His children. He wants us to listen to Him, but He also desires to hear from us, even about the seemingly trivial details of our lives, as is evident in this exchange between Him and the Apostle of Divine Mercy.

"Today, the Lord said to me, 'My daughter, I am told that there is much simplicity in you, so why do you not tell Me about everything that concerns you, even the smallest details? Tell me about everything, and know that this will give me great joy.' I answered, 'But you know about everything, Lord.' And Jesus replied to me, 'Yes, I do know; but you should not excuse yourself with the fact that I know, but with childlike simplicity talk to Me about everything, for My ears and heart are inclined towards you, and your words are dear to Me.'"

While Jesus wants an intimate relationship with us during our time on earth, His ultimate goal is to give us the gift of everlasting life, and he continually reminded Sister Faustina of this, urging her repeatedly to pray for the conversion of sinners. He also made numerous requests for the institution of Divine Mercy Sunday by the Church and said it would release a flood of blessings on humanity.

> My daughter, tell the whole world about my inconceivable mercy. I desire that the Feast of Mercy be a refuge and shelter for all souls, and especially for poor sinners. On that day the very depths of My tender mercy are open. I pour out a whole ocean of graces upon those souls who approach the fount of My mercy. The soul that will go to Confession and receive Holy Communion shall obtain complete forgiveness of sins and punishment. On that day all the divine floodgates through which grace flow are opened. Let no soul fear to draw near to Me, even though its sins be as scarlet. My mercy is so great that no mind, be it of man or of angel, will be able to fathom it throughout all eternity. Everything that exists has come forth from the very depths of My most tender mercy. Every soul in its relation to Me will contemplate My love and mercy throughout eternity. The Feast of Mercy

emerged from My very depths of
tenderness. It is my desire that it
be solemnly celebrated on the first
Sunday after Easter. Mankind will
not have peace until it turns to the
Fount of My Mercy.

On several occasions angels led the Apostle
of Divine Mercy to the depths of hell so she could
see the terrible suffering of those who reject
God's mercy completely. She described ghastly
torments the souls endured there and left a warn-
ing in her diary for skeptics.

> Today, I was led by an Angel to
> the chasms of hell. It is a place of
> great torture; how awesomely large
> and extensive it is! The kinds of
> tortures I saw: the first torture that
> constitutes hell is the loss of God;
> the second is perpetual remorse of
> conscience; the third is that one's
> condition will never change; the
> fourth is the fire that will penetrate
> the soul without destroying it—a
> terrible suffering, since it is a purely
> spiritual fire, lit by God's anger; the
> fifth torture is continual darkness
> and a terrible suffocating smell,
> and, despite the darkness, the dev-
> ils and the souls of the damned see

each other and all the evil, both
of others and their own; the sixth
torture is the constant company of
Satan; the seventh torture is horrible despair, hatred of God, vile
words, curses and blasphemies.
These are the tortures suffered by
all the damned together, but that
is not the end of the sufferings.
There are special tortures destined
for particular souls. These are the
torments of the senses. Each soul
undergoes terrible and indescribable sufferings, related to the manner in which it has sinned. There are
caverns and pits of torture where
one form of agony differs from
another. I would have died at the
very sight of these tortures if the
omnipotence of God had not sup-
ported me. Let the sinner know that
he will be tortured throughout all
eternity, in those senses he made
use of to sin. I am writing this at the
command of God, so that no soul
may find an excuse by saying there
is no hell, or that nobody has ever
been there, and so no one can say
what it is like.

I, Sister Faustina, by the order of
God, have visited the abysses of hell

so that I might tell souls about it and testify to its existence. I cannot speak about it now; but I have received a command from God to leave it in writing. The devils were full of hatred for me, but they had to obey me at the command of God. What I have written is but a pale shadow of the things I saw. But I noticed one thing: that most of the souls there are those who disbelieved that there is a hell. When I came to, I could hardly recover from the fright. How terribly souls suffer there!

While Jesus gave Saint Faustina the chaplet as a way to pray efficaciously, He told her that prayer was only one part of a fervent spiritual life.

My daughter, if I demand through you that people revere My mercy, you should be the first to distinguish yourself by this confidence in My mercy. I demand from you deeds of mercy, which are to arise out of love for Me. You are to show mercy to your neighbors always and everywhere. You must not shrink from this or try to excuse or absolve yourself from it.

I am giving you three ways of exercising mercy toward your neighbor: the first—by deed, the second—by word, the third—by prayer. In these three degrees is contained the fullness of mercy, and it is an unquestionable proof of love for Me. By this means a soul glorifies and pays reverence to My mercy. Yes, the first Sunday after Easter is the Feast of Mercy, but there also must be acts of mercy, and I demand the worship of My mercy through the solemn celebration of the Feast and through the veneration of the image which is painted. By means of this image I shall grant many graces to souls. It is to be a reminder of the demands of My mercy, because even the strongest faith is of no avail without works.

Merciful actions, merciful words and prayers all identify us as children of the Most High.

God told Sister Faustina that the Chaplet would be especially fruitful as a prayer for the dying. On numerous occasions she was given to understand that a particular soul was nearing the time of death and was in need of prayer. She sometimes prayed the chaplet spontaneously for that person. At other times God told her explicitly to pray the chaplet for a dying person. The Father of mercies reiterated how powerful the prayer is.

"At the hour of their death, I defend as My own glory every soul that will say this chaplet; or when others say it for a dying person, the indulgence is the same. When this chaplet is said by the bedside of a dying person, God's anger is placated, unfathomable mercy envelops the soul, and the very depths of My tender mercy are moved for the sake of the sorrowful Passion of My Son."

On Divine Mercy Sunday in 1937, Saint Faustina went to adoration, and God spoke to her again.

> My beloved daughter, write down these words, that today My Heart has rested in this convent [the Cracow house]. Tell the world about My mercy and My love.
>
> The flames of mercy are burning me. I desire to pour them out upon human souls. Oh, what pain they cause Me when they do not want to accept them!
>
> My daughter, do whatever is within your power to spread devotion to My mercy. I will make up for what you lack. Tell aching mankind

to snuggle close to My merciful Heart, and I will fill it with peace.

Tell [all people], My daughter, that I am Love and Mercy itself. When a soul approaches Me with trust, I fill it with such an abundance of graces that it cannot contain them within itself, but radiates them to other souls.

Souls who spread the honor of My mercy I shield through their entire lives as a tender mother her infant, and at the hour of death I will not be a Judge for them, but the Merciful Savior. At that last hour, a soul has nothing with which to defend itself except My mercy. Happy is the soul that during its life-time immersed itself in the Fountain of Mercy, because Justice will have no hold on it.

Write this: Everything that exists is enclosed in the bowels of My mercy, more deeply than an infant in its mother's womb. How painfully distrust of My goodness wounds Me! Sins of distrust wound Me most painfully.

One day Saint Faustina asked Jesus how He could tolerate so many sins, and why He did not punish sinners more. He said, "I have eternity for punishing [these], and so I am prolonging the time of mercy for the sake of [sinners]. But woe to them if they do not recognize this time of My visitation. My daughter, secretary of My mercy, your duty is not only to write about and proclaim My mercy, but also to beg for this grace for them, so that they too may glorify My mercy."

Jesus frequently told Saint Faustina that the greatest sinners had the greatest right to His mercy. "My daughter, write that the greater the misery of a soul, the greater its right to My mercy; [urge] all souls to trust in the unfathomable abyss of My mercy, because I want to save them all. On the cross, the fountain of My mercy was opened wide by the lance for all souls—no one have I excluded!"

In 1937 Jesus gave Sister Faustina a novena to pray. The novena was to begin on Good Friday and end the day before Divine Mercy Sunday. The following is the text as it appears in her diary. First are the words of God for each day, followed by a prayer Saint Faustina composed for each day.

> I desire that during these nine days you bring souls to the fount of My mercy, that they may draw therefrom strength and refreshment and whatever graces they need in the hardships of life and, especially, at the hour of death.

On each day you will bring to My Heart a different group of souls, and you will immerse them in this ocean of My mercy, and I will bring all these souls into the house of My Father. You will do this in this life and in the next. I will deny nothing to any soul whom you will bring to the fount of My mercy. On each day you will beg My Father, on the strength of My bitter Passion, for graces for these souls.

First Day

"Today, bring to Me all mankind, especially all sinners, and immerse them in the ocean of My mercy. In this way you will console Me in the bitter grief into which the loss of souls plunges Me."

Most Merciful Jesus, whose very nature it is to have compassion on us and to forgive us, do not look upon our sins, but upon the trust which we place in Your infinite goodness. Receive us all into the abode of Your Most Compassionate Heart, and never let us escape from It. We beg this of You by Your love which unites You to the Father and the Holy Spirit.

Oh omnipotence of Divine
Mercy,
Salvation of sinful people,
You are a sea of mercy and
compassion;
You aid those who entreat
You with humility.

Eternal Father, turn Your merciful gaze upon all mankind and especially poor sinners, all enfolded in the Most Compassionate Heart of Jesus. For the sake of His sorrowful Passion, show us Your mercy, that we may praise the omnipotence of Your mercy forever and ever. Amen.

Second Day

"Today bring to Me the souls of priests and religious, and immerse them in My unfathomable mercy. It was they who gave Me the strength to endure My bitter Passion. Through them, as through channels, My mercy flows out upon mankind."

Most Merciful Jesus, from whom comes all that is good, increase Your grace in us, that we may perform worthy works of mercy, and that all who see us may glorify the Father of Mercy who is in heaven.

The fountain of God's love
Dwells in pure hearts,
Bathed in the Sea of Mercy,
Radiant as stars, bright as
the dawn.

Eternal Father, turn Your merciful gaze upon the company [of chosen ones] in Your vineyard—upon the souls of priests and religious; and endow them with the strength of Your blessing. For the love of the Heart of Your Son, in which they are enfolded, impart to them Your power and light, that they may be able to guide others in the way of salvation, and with one voice sing praise to Your boundless mercy for ages without end. Amen.

Third Day

"Today bring to Me all devout and faithful souls, and immerse them in the ocean of My mercy. These souls brought Me consolation on the Way of the Cross. They were that drop of consolation in the midst of an ocean of bitterness."

Most Merciful Jesus, from the treasury of Your mercy, You impart Your graces in great abundance to each and all. Receive us into the abode of Your Most Compassionate Heart and never let us escape from It. We beg this of You by that most wondrous love for the heavenly Father with which Your Heart burns so fiercely.

> The miracles of mercy are impenetrable.
> Neither the sinner nor just one will fathom them.
> When you cast upon us an eye of pity,
> You draw us all closer to your love.

Eternal Father, turn Your merciful gaze upon faithful souls, as upon the inheritance of Your Son. For the sake of His sorrowful Passion, grant them Your blessing and surround them with your constant protection. Thus may they never fail in love or lose the treasure of the holy faith, but rather, with all the hosts of Angels and Saints, may they glorify Your boundless mercy for endless ages. Amen.

Fourth Day

"Today bring to me the pagans and those who do not yet know me. I was thinking also of them during My bitter Passion, and their future zeal comforted My Heart. Immerse them in the ocean of My mercy."

Most Compassionate Jesus, You are the Light of the whole world. Receive into the abode of Your Most Compassionate Heart the souls of pagans who as yet do not know You. Let the rays of Your grace enlighten them that they, too, together with us, may extol Your wonderful mercy; and do not let them escape from the abode which is Your Most Compassionate Heart.

> May the light of Your love
> Enlighten the souls in darkness;
> Grant that these souls will know You
> And, together with us, praise Your mercy.

Eternal Father, turn Your merciful gaze upon the souls of pagans and of those who as yet do not know You, but who are enclosed in the Most Compassionate Heart of Jesus. Draw them to the light of the Gospel. These souls do not know what great happiness it is to love You. Grant that they, too, may extol the generosity of Your mercy for endless ages. Amen.

Fifth Day

"Today bring to Me the souls of heretics and schismatics, and immerse them in the ocean of My mercy. During My bitter Passion they tore at My Body and Heart; that is, My Church. As they return to unity with the Church, My wounds heal, and in this way they alleviate My Passion."

Most Merciful Jesus, Goodness Itself, You do not refuse light to those who seek it of You. Receive into the abode of Your Most Compassionate Heart the souls of heretics and schismatics. Draw them by Your light into the unity of the Church, and do not let them escape from the abode of Your Most Compassionate Heart; but bring it about that they, too, come to adore the generosity of Your mercy.

Even for those who have torn the garment of Your unity,
A fount of mercy flows from Your Heart.
The omnipotence of Your mercy, Oh God,
Can lead these souls out of error.

Eternal Father, turn Your merciful gaze upon the souls of heretics and schismatics, who have squandered Your blessings and misused Your graces by obstinately persisting in their errors. Do not look upon their errors, but upon the love of Your own Son and upon His bitter Passion, which He underwent for their sake, since they, too, are enclosed in the Most Compassionate Heart of Jesus. Bring it about that they also may glorify Your great mercy for endless ages. Amen.

Sixth Day

"Today bring to Me the meek and humble souls and the souls of little children, and immerse them in My mercy. These souls most closely resemble My Heart. They strengthened Me during My bitter agony. I saw them as earthly Angels, who would keep vigil at My altars. I pour out upon them whole torrents of grace. Only the humble soul is able to receive My grace. I favor humble souls with My confidence."

Most merciful Jesus, You Yourself have said, "Learn from Me for I am meek and humble of Heart."

Receive into the abode of Your Most Compassionate Heart all meek and humble souls and the souls of little children. These souls send all heaven into ecstasy, and they are the heavenly Father's favorites. They are a sweet-smelling bouquet before the throne of God; God Himself takes delight in their fragrance. These souls have a permanent abode in Your Most Compassionate Heart, O Jesus, and they unceasingly sing out a hymn of love and mercy.

> A truly gentle and humble soul
> Already here on earth the air of paradise breathes,
> And in the fragrance of her humble heart
> The Creator Himself delights.

Eternal Father, turn Your merciful gaze upon meek and humble souls, and upon the souls of little children, who are enfolded in the abode which is the Most Compassionate Heart of Jesus. These souls bear the closest resemblance to Your Son. Their fragrance rises from the earth and reaches Your very throne. Father of mercy and of all goodness, I beg You by the love You bear these souls and by the delight You take in them: bless the whole world, that all souls together may sing out the praises of Your mercy for endless ages. Amen.

Seventh Day
"Today bring to Me the souls who especially venerate and glorify My mercy, and immerse them in My mercy. These souls sorrowed most over My Passion and entered Most deeply into My Spirit. They are living images of My Compassionate Heart. These souls will shine with a special brightness in the next life. Not one of them will go into the fire of hell. I shall particularly defend each one of them at the hour of death."

Most Merciful Jesus, whose Heart is Love Itself, receive into the abode of Your Most Compassionate Heart the souls of those who particularly extol and venerate the greatness of Your mercy. These souls are mighty with the very power of God Himself. In the midst of all afflictions and adversities they go forward, confident of Your mercy. These souls are united to Jesus and carry all mankind on their shoulders. These souls will not be judged severely, but Your mercy will embrace them as they depart from this life.

> A soul who praises the goodness of her Lord
> Is especially loved by Him.
> She is always close to the living fountain
> And draws graces from Mercy Divine.

Eternal Father, turn Your merciful gaze upon the souls who glorify and venerate Your greatest attribute, that of Your fathomless mercy, and who are enclosed in the Most Compassionate Heart of Jesus. These souls are a living Gospel; their hands are full of deeds of mercy, and their spirit, overflowing with joy, sings a canticle of mercy to You, O Most High! I beg You O God: Show them Your mercy according to the hope and trust they have placed in You. Let there be accomplished in them the promise of Jesus who said to them, "I Myself will defend as My own glory, during their lifetime, and especially at the hour of their death, those souls who will venerate My fathomless mercy."

Eighth Day

"Today bring to Me the souls who are in the prison of Purgatory, and immerse them in the abyss of My mercy. Let the torrents of My Blood cool down their scorching flames. All these souls are greatly loved by Me. They are making ret-ribution to My justice. It is in your power to bring them relief. Draw all the indulgences from the treasury of My Church and offer them on their behalf. Oh, if you only knew the torments they suffer, you would continually offer for them the alms of the spirit and pay off their debt to My justice."

Most Merciful Jesus, You Yourself have said that You desire mercy; so I bring into the abode of Your Most Compassionate Heart the souls in Purgatory, souls who are very dear to You, and yet, who must make retribution to Your justice. May the streams of Blood and Water which gushed forth from Your Heart put out the flames of the purifying fire, that in that place, too, the power of Your mercy may be praised.

> From the terrible heat of the cleansing fire
> Rises a plaint to Your mercy,
> And they receive comfort, refreshment, relief
> In the stream of mingled Blood and Water.

Eternal Father, turn Your merciful gaze upon the souls suffering in Purgatory, who are enfolded in the Most Compassionate Heart of Jesus. I beg You, by the sorrowful Passion of Jesus Your Son, and by all the bitterness with which His most sacred Soul was flooded, manifest Your mercy to the souls who are under Your just scrutiny. Look upon them in no other way than through the Wounds of Jesus, Your dearly beloved Son; for we firmly believe that there is no limit to Your goodness and compassion.

Ninth Day

"Today bring to Me souls who have become lukewarm, and immerse them in the abyss of My mercy. These souls wounded My Heart most painfully. My soul suffered the most dreadful loathing in the Garden of Olives because of lukewarm souls. They were the reason I cried out: 'Father, take this cup away from Me, if it be Your will.' For them, the last hope of salvation is to flee to My mercy."

Most Compassionate Jesus, You are Compassion Itself. I bring lukewarm souls into the abode of Your Most Compassionate Heart. In this fire of Your pure love let these tepid souls, who, like corpses, filled You with such deep loathing, be once again set aflame. O Most Compassionate Jesus, exercise the omnipotence of Your mercy and draw them into the very ardor of Your love; and bestow upon them the gift of holy love, for nothing is beyond Your power.

> Fire and ice cannot be joined;
> Either the fire dies, or the ice melts.
> But by Your mercy, O God,
> You can make up for all that is lacking.

Eternal Father, turn Your merciful gaze upon lukewarm souls, who are nonetheless enfolded in the Most Compassionate Heart of Jesus.

Father of Mercy, I beg You by the bitter Passion of Your Son and by His three-hour agony on the Cross: Let them, too, glorify the abyss of Your mercy.

Sister Faustina said in her diary that Jesus instructed her to write down the words of this novena. The text has been translated into many languages, and people all over the world now make the novena every year, beginning on Good Friday. Many people also recite the Chaplet of Divine Mercy each day during the novena.

Another rich spiritual practice given to the world through Sister Faustina is the observance of a moment of prayer each day to mark the time Jesus died on the cross. Jesus asked her to observe this practice, and many other people have since adopted it as well.

"At three o'clock, implore My mercy, especially for sinners; and, if only for a brief moment, immerse yourself in My Passion, particularly in My abandonment at the moment of agony. I will allow you to enter into My mortal sorrow. I will refuse nothing to the soul that makes a request of Me in virtue of My Passion," Jesus said.

On another occasion Jesus returned to this topic and gave Saint Faustina specific suggestions about how to observe the hour of mercy. He said,

I remind you, My daughter, that as often as you hear the clock strike the third hour, immerse yourself completely in My mercy, adoring and glorifying it; invoke its omnipotence for the whole world, and particularly for poor sinners; for at that moment mercy was opened wide for every soul. In this hour you can obtain everything for yourself and for others for the asking; it was the hour of grace for the whole world— mercy triumphed over justice.

My daughter, try your best to make the Stations of the Cross in this hour, provided that your duties permit it; and if you are not able to make the Stations of the Cross, then at least step into the chapel for a moment and adore, in the Blessed Sacrament, My Heart, which is full of mercy; and should you be unable to step into the chapel, immerse yourself in prayer there where you happen to be, if only for a very brief instant.

This observance is now practiced throughout the world, as people pause momentarily to remember God's tremendous gift of mercy. And because it takes only a moment, it can be practiced anywhere. Some people spend part of this hour in prayer.

While Jesus recommended these specific practices, He also emphasized the need for people to take advantage of the great graces available in the sacrament of confession.

> Write, speak of My mercy. Tell souls where they are to look for solace; that is, in the Tribunal of Mercy [the Sacrament of Reconciliation]. There the greatest miracles take place [and] are incessantly repeated. To avail oneself of this miracle, it is not necessary to go on a great pilgrimage or to carry out some external ceremony; it suffices to come with faith to the feet of My representative and to reveal to him one's misery, and the miracle of Divine Mercy will be fully demonstrated. Were a soul like a decaying corpse so that from a human standpoint, there would be no [hope of] restoration and everything would already be lost, it is not so with God. The miracle of Divine Mercy restores that soul in full. Oh, how miserable are those who do not take advantage of the miracle

> of God's mercy! You will call out in
> vain, but it will be too late.

Despite the fact that she was the recipient of such extraordinary graces, Saint Faustina lived what appeared to be an ordinary life within her Congregation. She worked with the girls and young women; sometimes she worked in the kitchen, sometimes in the garden. Her superiors knew of the extraordinary events, but Saint Faustina typically kept silence about her unusual experiences, which included locutions, visions, a hidden stigmata and mystical marriage to Jesus. Although some of the other sisters realized that Saint Faustina was an extraordinarily holy woman, many regarded her as a bit of an eccentric, and some even accused her of exaggerating illnesses as a way to be excused from the hard manual labor the sisters shared.

Father Sopocko took the lead in publicizing the Divine Mercy image and other elements of the devotion, arranging for the publication of holy cards and pamphlets to introduce people to the various prayers and practices. Saint Faustina rejoiced at the spread of the devotion even as she suffered from declining health as a result of tuberculosis. She died in Cracow on October 5, 1938. She was thirty-three years old.

The Divine Mercy devotion spread rapidly in Poland and Lithuania during World War II, and the Congregation of Marians of the Immaculate Conception introduced it in the United States during that time.

It appeared to suffer a complete reversal in 1958 and 1959, however, when the Vatican forbade the spread of the devotion in its then current form. The Holy See took this action after a review of Sister Faustina's diary. Only years later would it become clear that somehow a tragically erroneous translation of the diary had been the basis for this decision.

But God had other plans.

In 1965 Bishop Julian Groblicki, under the direction of Archbishop Karol Wojtyla (the future Pope John Paul II), opened the Informative Process to assess the life and virtues of Sister Faustina. The process was completed in 1967 and received in Rome the following year.

In April of 1978, in light of newer and more accurate translations of Sister Faustina's diary, the ban on the Divine Mercy devotion was lifted at the request of Cardinal Wojtyla of Cracow. On October 16 of that year, Cardinal Wojtyla was elected the pope. It was the Feast of Saint Margaret Mary.

While some people have drawn distinctions between the devotions to the Sacred Heart and the Divine Mercy, John Paul appeared to see them as essentially one. He was a great promoter of devotion to the Heart of Jesus in whatever form. John Paul presented a beautiful series of meditations on the Litany of the Sacred Heart. He also made frequent references in his homilies to Divine Mercy.

John Paul the Great beatified Sister Faustina on April 18, 1993, Divine Mercy Sunday. Then, on April 30, 2000, Divine Mercy Sunday for that year, he presided over her canonization, making her the first saint of the new millennium.

Millions of pilgrims have traveled to the Divine Mercy shrine in Cracow. Many people have received extraordinary blessings from God in the convent's chapel while kneeling before the Divine Mercy image there. Jesus once told Sister Faustina that His gaze from the image is like His gaze from the cross. One might take His words to mean that it would be a look of anguish, distress or even condemnation. However, the gaze from the image is one of infinite tenderness. Jesus, full of compassionate love, frees us from paralyzing distrust. The exquisite rays emanating from His Sacred Heart encompass the whole world, providing graces of repentance, renewal, hope and joy.

Part 2

Elements of Devotion

Seven

The Eucharist

I am the Lord your God,
who brought you up out of the land
of Egypt.
Open wide your mouth, and I will
fill it.
      Psalm 81:10

Shout, and sing for joy, O inhabitant
of Zion,
for great in your midst is the Holy
One of Israel.
      Isaiah 12:6

Do not labor for the food which
perishes, but for the food which
endures to eternal life, which the
Son of man will give to you; for on
him has God the Father set his seal.
      John 6:27

Jesus instituted the Blessed Sacrament the night before He died. This farewell gift to His disciples, which was one of His greatest miracles, expressed the intense ambivalence erupting within His Sacred Heart. While He yearned to return to His Father, He couldn't bear to be away from His disciples; He wanted it both ways. And so it was that the Son of Man became real food, the Bread of Life, for us. Jesus looked out across the ages and saw the millions of people who would receive Him and be nourished by His inestimable holiness. He saw how many would achieve a perfect love of Him by sharing in this sacred meal, and He rejoiced.

The Eucharist is one of the primary means Jesus uses to pour out the treasures of His Sacred Heart on humanity. Jesus once told Saint Gertrude that these riches are so vast that waves of grace sweep through the universe and beyond it every time anyone receives Communion. Blessings rain down on everyone on earth, the suffering of every soul in purgatory is reduced and every citizen of heaven experiences increased joy. The fierce love of Jesus expresses itself so powerfully through this sacrament that its effects are beyond measure.

This precious food our adorable Savior offers us is, in some ways, the opposite of earthly food. We are accustomed to eating food and being nourished as we digest it; food becomes a source of energy and well-being for us as we absorb it and make it part of ourselves. The Body and Blood of Christ do indeed do this, but they also work in another way. The food and drink Jesus offers nourish us by absorbing us more profoundly into the Mystical Body of Christ. Graces we receive when Jesus enters our hearts and souls through the Eucharist enable us to break away from sin and become pure. We share in the transubstantiation of humanity through Communion with the Heart of Jesus.

The nature of the Blessed Sacrament teaches us much about Jesus and His ardent love for us. The Eucharist was instituted at a Passover Seder. This heavenly food can free us from the destruction of sinfulness just as dramatically as the people of Israel were delivered from the angel of death, who brought such devastation to the Egyptians. The first Passover was a demonstration of God's willingness to take the most drastic steps to lead His people out of bondage and into the exquisitely beautiful country He had prepared for them. The night of miracles signaled the beginning of a long journey. In the same way, the Eucharist provides us with a way to escape bondage to selfishness and sin, and gives nourishment for our journey to the Father and the paradise He has prepared for us.

Jesus chose bread and wine to make Himself available to everyone because these foods can be found throughout the world and among all classes of people. Indeed, it may be that God originally created grain and grapes for this purpose. His choice of such common elements illustrates a further sign of His humility, which He already displayed by deigning to become a member of the human race. Jesus places Himself in our hands through the Eucharist and offers us an exchange of hearts. He allows us to place our hearts and our entire lives in His holy hands as we receive Him. The graces that issue from the Sacred Heart in the Eucharist make it possible for us to trust God with our lives, abandoning ourselves to His will.

What He wants most is an intimate union with us, and the Blessed Sacrament offers a most efficacious way to achieve that union. A soul Jesus Himself has caressed has every opportunity to destroy anything that prevents complete immersion in God's grace. This is why devotion to the Sacred Heart of Jesus and the Eucharist are so intimately intertwined. The Eucharist is at the center of this devotion, just as the glorious Heart of Jesus, aflame with a tender and passionate love for us, is at the center of the Eucharist.

One of the most eloquent statements of this truth is found in *The Book of Infinite Love* by Mother Louise Margaret Claret de la Touche (1868–1915). This holy member of the Visitation order received many revelations from God about the Sacred Heart of Jesus, focusing on the relationship between the Sacred Heart and the priesthood. In one section she wrote the following about the Eucharist:

> The devotion to the Blessed Eucharist and the devotion to the Sacred Heart are not only two sister devotions, in reality, they are only one and the same devotion. They complete each other and develop each other; they blend so perfectly together that one cannot stand without the other, and their union is absolute. Not only can one of these devotions not be prejudicial to the other but, because they complete each other and perfect each other, they also reciprocally increase each other.
>
> If we have devotion to the Sacred Heart, we will wish to find It, to adore It, to love It, to offer It our reparation and praise, and where shall we look for It but in the Blessed Eucharist where It is found eternally living?
>
> If we love this adorable Heart, we will wish to unite ourselves to It, for love seeks union, we will wish to warm our hearts by the ardour of this divine fire, but to reach the Sacred Heart, to take hold of It, to

put It in contact with our own, what shall we do? Shall we scale heaven to bear away the Heart of Jesus Who reigns triumphant in glory? There is no need to do so.

We will go to the Blessed Eucharist, we will go to the tabernacle, we will take the white Host, and when we have enclosed it in our breast, we will feel the divine Heart truly beating beside our own.

We are called to a deep and eternal gratitude to our Savior for instituting the Blessed Sacrament. Jesus invites us to show this gratitude in many ways. First, He asks us to remove any obstacles to His grace by making frequent use of the sacrament of confession. The Sacred Heart is a boundless ocean of mercy for sinners. Jesus yearns to forgive our sins and bring us into an unblemished relationship with the Father. Confession is also an act of humility in that it forces us to confront our failures. We become more like Christ—who described Himself as gentle and humble of Heart—through acts of humility, and in so doing we grow closer to Him. God expresses His glory and power through love and mercy. The graces available through the sacrament of mercy can help us to overcome faults that would otherwise become serious obstacles to having a close relationship with Him.

God asks that we prepare ourselves for confession through an examination of conscience, but we do not have to be excessively scrupulous. Saint Margaret Mary once found herself feeling anxious about making a good confession, but Jesus told her not to be anxious, using these words: "Why dost thou torment thyself? Do what lies in thy power, I will supply what is wanting. In this Sacrament I ask for nothing so much as for a contrite and humble heart which, with a sincere will never to offend Me again, accuses itself frankly. I then pardon without delay, and hence follows perfect amendment."

We can also prepare to receive the Eucharist through prayers of praise and thanksgiving. If we were planning to receive a world-famous guest at our homes, we would spare no effort or expense to get ready for the big event. Through prayer we can prepare to receive Jesus and become renewed temples of the Holy Spirit. We can praise God for creating this miraculous sacrament of love and thank Him for the opportunity to receive Him. We can also pray for all those on earth and in purgatory who yearn to receive the Eucharist but are unable to do so, asking God to bless them generously.

Most people receive Communion at Mass or a Communion service except for unusual circumstances involving an illness. We can prepare to receive Jesus by offering prayers of thanksgiving for the gift of the Eucharist before we set off for Mass. The celebrant plays a critical role in the

Sacrament of the Altar, and praying for the priest who will celebrate Mass is a good practice as well. We can offer prayers of thanksgiving for the priest's vocation and more prayers asking that the homily will spring from the guidance and inspiration of the Holy Spirit.

The scripture readings for Mass are chosen carefully for each day of the year and together form a mosaic of God's love for us. Praying to the Holy Spirit for the ability to understand the scriptures that we hear and read brings great blessings. Another practice that enhances participation at Mass is to imagine that the scriptures are coming from the mouth of God, Who is speaking them for the first time. This helps participants to pay close attention to God's revelations and is another way to prepare for the Eucharistic feast that follows the readings.

The consecration is a moment of incomparable holiness and wonder. We can pray to the Blessed Mother and Saint Joseph, asking them to help us witness the entrance of Jesus into our midst in the same spirit of awe that prevailed at His nativity. Saint Gertrude once found herself about to receive the Eucharist without having made much preparation. She offered God the merits of the Blessed Mother and the saints, including the works they had performed to prepare themselves to receive His graces, because she felt she had little to offer herself. God accepted these merits as if they had come from Gertrude herself. This illustrates one of the remarkable traits of the devotion to the Sacred Heart. We are blessed even more as we practice it and take advantage of the communion of saints.

On another occasion Saint Gertrude received a revelation during the consecration at the moment when the host was elevated. God led her to understand that anyone who assists at Mass with devotion, trying to concentrate on Him, receives a special blessing at the consecration. The Father looks on these souls with the same tenderness with which He regards the consecrated host.

Receiving Communion is a blessing, but it involves responsibility as well. How are we to act when we receive our God? And how are we to behave after we have received Him and are carrying Him within us? Again, asking Mary to intercede for us is a great help. The Blessed Mother carried Jesus within her for nine months, and she prays fervently for anyone who asks for help in learning how to live in a way that gives glory to God. One change that comes about when we allow God's grace free movement within us through the Eucharist is a stronger spirit of generosity and charity toward our neighbors. Saint Margaret Mary gave this advice: "You should never find fault with, accuse or judge anyone but yourself, so that your lips that are destined to praise God, and your tongue on which the Sacred Host so often rests, may not serve Satan as instruments to sully your soul."

We have a few moments alone with the Lord after we receive the Eucharist and return to our place in church. This can be an occasion of thanksgiving and adoration, a time to petition for favors or simply a quiet opportunity to listen to the rapturous rhythms of the Sacred Heart within us. The end of Mass and our departure from church need not mark the end of our Eucharistic banquet, and Jesus delights in our efforts when we remain in a prayerful state of mind after leaving. One worthwhile practice is to make an effort to be mindful of the presence of Jesus within us during the first hour after we receive Him. This is pleasing to Him and helps to form the habit of being aware of God's presence.

Jesus once told Saint Faustina that many people lose graces because they rush off to do other things too quickly after receiving Him. "I desire to unite Myself with human souls; My great delight is to unite Myself with souls. Know, My daughter, that when I come to a human heart in Holy Communion, My hands are full of all kinds of graces which I want to give to the soul. But souls do not even pay any attention to Me; they leave Me to Myself and busy themselves with other things. Oh, how sad I am that souls do not recognize Love! They treat Me as a dead object."

Jesus made the frequent reception of Communion a centerpiece of the devotion to His Sacred Heart when He revealed Himself to Saint Margaret Mary. He asked her to encourage

everyone to receive the Eucharist on nine consecutive first Fridays in honor of His Passion and
the sweet blessings of His Sacred Heart. Jesus
said that all those who fulfilled this request
would receive the grace of final repentance.
They wouldn't die in mortal sin or without having received their sacraments; they would find
a place of secure refuge within His Heart at
the hour of death. This promise of salvation is
designed to win souls by the excessive mercy the
Lord extends to those who make even the smallest efforts to love and honor Him. Jesus revealed
this to Margaret Mary when a heresy known as
Jansenism afflicted the church. Jansenism, which
has since been eradicated, discouraged people
from receiving Communion frequently. Christ
asks us to do just the opposite. While receiving
the Eucharist on first Fridays results in immeasurable benefits, God asks us to draw ever closer to
Him by receiving Him on other days as well. He
encourages us to receive Communion as often
as possible, not just on Sundays or Fridays. The
Sacred Heart of Jesus calls us to a growing union
with God.

Jesus yearns for our love so much that He
even blesses our desires for Communion. Saint
Margaret Mary related an incident that took
place on a Good Friday. "Having a great longing to receive Our Lord, with many tears I spoke
these words to Him: 'Loving Jesus, I want to be
consumed in desiring You, and not being able

to receive You today, I shall none the less keep on desiring You.' Thereupon He came to console me with His sweet presence, saying to me: 'My daughter, your desire has pierced My Heart so deeply that if I had not already instituted the Sacrament of love, I would do so now to become your food. I take such great pleasure in this longing that, as often as a heart forms this desire for Me, I look upon it lovingly to draw it to Myself.'"

Thus, devotion to the Sacred Heart sanctifies our good desires. Moreover, it includes a solution to one of the most vexing problems Catholics can face. Many people find that after receiving the Eucharist many times, the practice becomes routine and has little impact on their lives outside church. God sometimes removes the warm feelings we associate with the Eucharist to encourage us to attach ourselves directly to Him instead of to feelings or sensations we have come to associate with Him.

Still, those who regularly receive Communion but fail to make any progress in breaking away from habitual sin are in danger because they have received the supreme remedy for such afflictions. This failure to grow in grace and perseverance can be solved through prayer, particularly by directing prayers to the Sacred Heart before receiving Communion or while visiting the Blessed Sacrament. One of the finest fruits of this devotion is that the fire of the Heart of Jesus inflames lukewarm souls. Disciples of the

Sacred Heart become fervent souls, sometimes experiencing a passionate love for God they lost for years. They often receive a desire to love and serve Jesus that surpasses anything they ever experienced before.

While receiving Jesus at Mass is a significant step in creating a closer relationship with Him, visiting Him at other times is also important. Shortly after Jesus instituted the Eucharist, His friends and disciples abandoned Him, and He spent part of the night alone. His Sacred Heart grieved at this abandonment and the terrible solitude that would follow throughout the centuries.

The Son of God, Who is present in all the tabernacles of the world, is often left alone. Many hours pass during the day and night when no one comes to worship Him, praise Him, thank Him or simply spend a few minutes keeping Him company. The irony of this situation is beyond measure. Here is the Lord of the universe, making Himself and His boundless graces available to His people; here are His people, ignoring Him. Jesus once described this situation to Saint Margaret Mary with these words: "I thirst with such a terrible thirst to be loved by men in the Blessed Sacrament that this thirst consumes Me. Yet I find no one trying to quench it according to My desire by some return of My love."

Jesus made Himself a prisoner of the tabernacle to be with as many of His disciples as possible as often as possible. Yet few people take advantage of this opportunity, and our Holy Redeemer is often left as alone as He was on the night before His death. The easiest way to correct this problem is to treat Jesus at least as well as we would treat any other friend. We don't limit our association with close friends to only a token hour or so a week. We spend time with them as often as possible, sometimes planning ahead but also enjoying more spontaneous visits. While we may enjoy getting together with a group of friends, we also relish the intimacy of a one-on-one conversation. Sometimes we seek the company of friends for consolation in our difficulties, but we also share joys and successes. In addition, often we get together with our friends simply because we enjoy their companionship.

Jesus is delighted when we visit Him. Anyone who regularly spends time with Him by visiting one of the tabernacles where He dwells will find that it is often during these intimate moments that He chooses to speak to our hearts. Indeed, many well-known saints and untold numbers of other people have received extraordinary graces from the Sacred Heart of Jesus while adoring the Blessed Sacrament. This can also be a time to obtain graces for others. Saint Margaret Mary would sometimes "kneel in" for another soul by placing herself before the Blessed Sacrament. She would ask Jesus to give all the merits of her time spent with Him and her adoration of Him to someone else, reserving nothing for herself. These and other acts of charity have earned her a unique place in heaven.

Our visits to the Blessed Sacrament can be filled with variety and spontaneity. We can go before the Sacred Heart of Jesus just to thank Him for being present in all the tabernacles of the world. Or we can ask for a healing or other blessing for ourselves or for others. Jesus welcomes our prayers, whatever they may be, and delights in our efforts to spend time with Him. A visit to the Blessed Sacrament can be a time of intense praise or a few moments of peaceful gratitude. We can talk or just listen. Those who practice contemplative forms of prayer will find no better setting. Charismatic prayer groups that meet in a church or chapel with a tabernacle enjoy praising God where He is present in a special way. Every moment spent in adoration before the Blessed Sacrament will be rewarded with an infinite number of blessings in eternity.

And our visits to Jesus in the Blessed Sacrament give Him the opportunity to strengthen us and console us as we perform our duties in life. Saint Teresa of the Andes addressed this point in a letter to her father. "How your life would change if you went to Him often as a Friend. Can you be thinking Jesus won't want to welcome you as a friend? If that's what you thought, it would be a sign you don't know Him. Jesus is all tenderness, all love for His sinful creatures. He lives in the tabernacle with His Heart open to receive us, waiting for our arrival that He may console us."

Devotion to the Sacred Heart also offers us an opportunity to offer perfect prayers to the Father. Our requests, thanks and praise become sanctified in the flames of love when we unite our prayers to those the Heart of Jesus offers for us in the Blessed Sacrament. The Sacred Heart is a purifying furnace, and everything Jesus offers to the Father is eternally pleasing to Him. This is one of the greatest blessings Jesus bestowed on humanity by revealing the mysteries of His Heart to us. A person offering a prayer may be lacking in humility or insufficiently fervent, but a prayer offered through the Sacred Heart is transformed into a delightful song of love before rising to the Father.

The word *Eucharist* means "thanksgiving" or "gratitude." Devotion to the Sacred Heart in the Eucharist is both a means of expressing our thanks to God for all His blessings and a way of living in a spirit of gratitude. Anyone touched by the Eucharist and open to the grace of God will grow more sensitive and aware of all the gifts the Holy Trinity has granted and will grant to humanity. A soul that becomes suffused with the graces of adoration will become much more inclined to thank Jesus for His Passion and all the blessings that have flowed from His pierced Heart throughout the ages. The birth of this spirit of gratitude is one of many changes that take place in disciples of the Sacred Heart, and it is a way in which the

devotion helps us to have a more balanced prayer
life. Many people, especially those afflicted with
troubles, find that they spend most of their prayer
time offering petitions for themselves. One of the
fruits of the devotion is a richer prayer life that
includes intercession for other people on earth
and in purgatory, praise, thanksgiving, repentance and adoration. The result is a more varied
and balanced relationship with God.

Friendship with the Sacred Heart centered in
the Eucharist transforms people and has implications on a community and global level as well.
Our views of our neighbors change as we start
to see them as members of the Mystical Body of
Christ, in whom the Eucharistic fullness of Jesus
is at work. We come to see the radiant presence
of the risen Christ in our neighbors and see our
neighbors alive in God. Eventually these blessings extend to all our neighbors, including those
of other faiths and those who have no faith.
The divine presence that dwells in the Eucharist
blesses the entire earth and all its inhabitants. We
grow more likely to think and act charitably and
become less prone to commit or condone acts
of violence as we come to a fuller realization of
God's Communion with His people.

***

We live in a world where Jesus Himself is present
on our altars, in tabernacles and in His people. He

calls to us from churches and chapels, from the hearts of our friends and the souls of strangers. "I am the resurrection and the life," He says. And the words that He spoke before calling Lazarus out of the tomb are repeated as He calls each of us out of the darkness of sin, the entombment that brings death to the soul. "Come out!" He cries. Come forth from the tomb of selfishness into the blazing light of day, a day illuminated by a pure and holy fire bursting from the Heart that has conquered death. This Heart was opened by a lance for you. This Heart is your rightful home. Come here for your sustenance, your rest and your hope. Come when you are joyful and when you mourn. It is open to you. Immerse yourselves in the Divine Mercy you find here. Behold the fountains of living waters that spring eternally here; empty yourselves and be filled with the living waters, and your souls will become like exquisite flowers kept in perpetual bloom. Drink of the Precious Blood and inherit eternal life.

"Come to me, all you who labor and are burdened, and I will give you rest. Take my yoke upon you and learn from me, for I am meek and humble of heart; and you will find rest for yourselves. For my yoke is easy, and my burden light."

Come into radiant union with Me. Come into My Sacred Heart, where all things are made easy, where all burdens are light. There is a place for you here, a place that has been reserved for you since before the universe existed, for I have loved you with an everlasting love. I have waited for you since before the beginning of time, preparing this place for you. Come now and take your place in this refuge of mercy and be sheltered in this life and the next. You will not find rest anywhere else, because this place of purification and sanctity is your true home.

Eucharistic Prayers

Prayer to the Father

Heavenly Father, we thank You for the gift of Your Son, and we praise You for Your infinite generosity. Help us to live in a spirit of gratitude by becoming Eucharistic souls, joined in Holy Communion to the Sacred Heart of Jesus. Bless our efforts to come to You and offer You our thanks through this glorious Heart. Let us be inflamed with the sanctifying fire that bursts eternally from the Heart of Your Son so that through His grace we may become pure enough to dwell before Your throne in heaven.

Prayer to Jesus

Lord Jesus, we praise You for Your glory and for all Your wondrous deeds. We thank You for enriching the earth and the entire human race by being present in all the tabernacles of the world. Please take our hearts and make them Your own. Pour the riches of Your Sacred Heart into our own hearts and souls, and help us to become the disciples You want us to be. Lord, by ourselves we are incapable of loving You the way You deserve to be loved. Let the sacred fire of Your pierced Heart inflame us. Grant us a tremendous outpouring of Your perfect love when we receive Your Body and Blood. Help us to return Your love, loving You with our whole hearts, our whole souls, our whole minds and all our strength. Give us the ardent charity You have for our brothers and sisters throughout the world so we can love and serve them as we should.

Prayer to the Holy Spirit

Holy Spirit, sweet Holy Spirit, we beg You to grant us new life through a renewal of Your graces, gifts and fruit in our lives. Come with Your power and wisdom to inspire us and guide us as we strive to become pure temples of Your love. Comfort us in our afflictions and help us to unite our sufferings and hardships with the glorious Passion of the Lamb of God. Help us to turn away from sin and become sanctified by Your presence so we may become pure enough to enter the Sacred Heart of our Lord and Savior, Jesus Christ, dwelling there in time and for eternity.

Prayer to the Blessed Mother

Holy Queen of Peace, please intercede for us so we may learn how to receive Jesus. Help us to prepare ourselves to consume your divine Son in the Eucharist and be consumed by His eternal love for us. Obtain for us the grace of humility that we may be awed by the Body and Blood of Jesus. Obtain for us the grace of obedience that we may conform ourselves to His perfect will. Help us to grow in charity that we may love and serve Him and His people. And help us to experience true joy as we become more mindful of His love for us.

Prayer to Saint Margaret Mary

St. Margaret Mary, glorious Apostle of the Sacred Heart of Jesus, we thank you for your tireless efforts on earth and in heaven to make the Son of God known and loved. Please pray for us that we may become true disciples of the Sacred Heart, transformed by the Eucharistic presence of Christ on earth. Obtain for us the courage and graces that we need to abandon ourselves to God's holy will, plunging ourselves into the pierced Heart of the Most High God to obtain mercy, love, peace and joy. We pray that these gifts may flourish in our lives so we, in turn, might bring them to others.

Eight

The Litany of the Sacred Heart

Pray for those who persecute you.
>   Matthew 5:44

Pray constantly.
>   1 Thessalonians 5:17

The prayer of a righteous man has great power in its effects.
>   James 5:16

M any of the formal prayers associated with the Sacred Heart reflect the biblical character of the devotion. Perhaps the best example is the beautiful Litany of the Sacred Heart of Jesus. In this prayer we find echoes of the words of saints who have promoted the Sacred Heart devotion, such as Margaret Mary, Francis de Sales and John Eudes. Yet the writings of Saint Gertrude the

Great, who studied the scriptures almost every day, and Mechthild of Hackeborn inspired much of this prayer. Gertrude had a great gift for understanding and explaining the Bible, and she was so immersed in scripture studies that many of her writings are full of quotations from the Bible and paraphrases of scriptural passages.

The Litany evolved over the years, and Pope Leo XIII approved the current form in 1899. It would become a favorite prayer of Saint John Paul II. Indeed, John Paul gave a series of Angelus meditations on the Litany beginning in 1985, which he completed in 1989. Prior to beginning this series of Angelus meditations—one of the most extensive of his papacy on a single topic—John Paul devoted an Angelus message to the Litany in 1982. Here John Paul, the great lover and promoter of the Sacred Heart devotion, recommended that the faithful pray the Litany in a deep, meditative fashion.

> It is a marvelous prayer, totally concentrated on the interior mystery of Christ, the God-Man. The Litany to the Heart of Jesus draws abundantly from biblical sources, and at the same time reflects the deepest experiences of human hearts. It is also a prayer of veneration and authentic dialogue.

In it we speak of the Heart, and we also allow our hearts to speak with this unique Heart that is the "fountain of life and holiness" and the "desire of the everlasting hills," with the Heart that is "patient and most merciful," enriching all who call upon him.

This prayer, recited and meditated, becomes a true school of the interior life, the school of the Christian.

The Solemnity of the Sacred Heart of Jesus reminds us above all of the moment when this Heart was "pierced with a lance" and by this piercing was visibly opened to humankind and to the world.

Reciting the litany—and in general venerating the Divine Heart—we learn the mystery of redemption in all its divine and human depth.

At the same time we become sensitive to the need for reparation. Christ opens his Heart to us that we may join him in his reparation for the salvation of the world. The language of the pierced Heart speaks the whole truth about his gospel and about Easter.

Let us try to understand this language ever better.

The full text of the Litany is presented here, followed by examples of how each of the thirty-three invocations related to the Heart of Christ has biblical components.

Lord, have mercy on us.
Christ, have mercy on us.
Lord, have mercy on us.
Christ, hear us.
Christ, graciously hear us.
God, the Father of heaven, have mercy on us.
God the Son, Redeemer of the world, have mercy on us ("have mercy on us" is repeated after each invocation).
God the Holy Spirit,
Holy Trinity, one God,
Heart of Jesus, Son of the eternal Father,
Heart of Jesus, formed by the Holy Spirit in the Virgin Mother's womb,
Heart of Jesus, substantially united to the Word of God,
Heart of Jesus, of infinite majesty,
Heart of Jesus, holy temple of God,
Heart of Jesus, tabernacle of the Most High,

Heart of Jesus, house of God and gate of heaven,

Heart of Jesus, glowing furnace of charity,

Heart of Jesus, vessel of justice and love,

Heart of Jesus, full of goodness and love,

Heart of Jesus, abyss of all virtues,

Heart of Jesus, most worthy of all praise,

Heart of Jesus, King and center of all hearts,

Heart of Jesus, wherein are all the treasures of wisdom and knowledge,

Heart of Jesus, wherein dwells all the fullness of the Godhead,

Heart of Jesus, in whom the Father is well pleased,

Heart of Jesus, of whose fullness we have all received,

Heart of Jesus, desire of the everlasting hills,

Heart of Jesus, patient and rich in mercy,

Heart of Jesus, rich unto all who call upon you,

Heart of Jesus, fount of life and holiness,

Heart of Jesus, propitiation for our offenses,

Heart of Jesus, overwhelmed with reproaches,

Heart of Jesus, bruised for our iniquities,

Heart of Jesus, obedient even unto death,

Heart of Jesus, pierced with a lance,

Heart of Jesus, source of all consolation,

Heart of Jesus, our life and resurrection,

Heart of Jesus, our peace and reconciliation,

Heart of Jesus, victim for our sins,

Heart of Jesus, salvation of those who hope in You,

Heart of Jesus, hope of those who die in You,

Heart of Jesus, delight of all the saints,

Lamb of God, who takes away the sins of the world, spare us, O Lord.

Lamb of God, who takes away the sins of the world, graciously hear us, O Lord.

Lamb of God, who takes away the sins of the world, have mercy on us.

V. Jesus meek and humble of heart.

R. Make our hearts like unto thine.

Scriptural Sources of the Litany

"Heart of Jesus, Son of the eternal Father, have mercy on us."

"Pray then like this:
   Our Father who art in heaven,
   Hallowed be thy name" (Matt. 6:9).

"Simon Peter replied, 'You are the Christ, the Son of the living God'" (Matt. 16:16).

"Father, I desire that they also, whom thou hast given me, may be with me where I am, to behold my glory which thou hast given me in thy love for me before the foundation of the world" (John 17:24).

***

"Heart of Jesus, formed by the Holy Spirit in the Virgin Mother's womb, have mercy on us."

"Therefore the Lord himself will give you a sign. Behold, a young woman shall conceive and bear a son, and shall call his name Immanuel" (Isa. 7:14).

"In the sixth month the angel Gabriel was sent from God to a city of Galilee named Nazareth, to a virgin betrothed to a man whose name was Joseph, of the house of David; and the virgin's name was Mary…And the angel said to her,
   The Holy Spirit will come upon you,
   and the power of the Most High will
   overshadow you;

therefore the child to be born will
be called holy,
the Son of God" (Luke 1:26–27, 35).

"Behold, the angel of the Lord appeared to him in a dream, saying, 'Joseph, son of David, do not fear to take Mary your wife, for that which is conceived in her is of the Holy Spirit'" (Matt. 1:20).

***

"Heart of Jesus, substantially united to the Word of God, have mercy on us."

"In the beginning was the Word, and the Word was with God, and the Word was God...And the Word became flesh and dwelt among us, full of grace and truth; we have beheld his glory, glory as of the only Son from the Father" (John 1:1, 14).

"That which was from the beginning, which we have heard, which we have seen with our eyes, which we have looked upon and touched with our hands, concerning the word of life—the life was made manifest, and we saw it, and testify to it, and proclaim to you the eternal life which was with the Father and was made manifest to us— that which we have seen and heard we proclaim also to you, so that you may have fellowship with us; and our fellowship is with the Father and with his Son Jesus Christ" (1 John 1:1–3).

"He is clad in a robe dipped in blood, and the name by which he is called is The Word of God" (Rev. 19:13).

***

"Heart of Jesus, of infinite majesty, have mercy on us."

"Your divine throne endures for ever and ever" (Ps. 45:6).

"Honor and majesty are before him; strength and beauty are in his sanctuary" (Ps. 96:6).

"Praise him for his mighty deeds; praise him according to his exceeding greatness!" (Ps. 150:2).

"For the Son of man is to come with his angels in the glory of his Father...You will see the Son of man seated at the right hand of Power, and coming on the clouds of heaven" (Matt. 16:27; 26:64).

"He is the image of the invisible God, the first-born of all creation" (Col. 1:15).

"In many and various ways God spoke of old to our fathers by the prophets; but in these last days he has spoken to us by a Son, whom he appointed the heir of all things, through whom also he created the world. He reflects the glory of God and bears the very stamp of his nature, upholding the universe by his word of power. When he had made purification for sins, he sat down at the right hand of the Majesty on high, having become as much superior to angels as the name he has obtained is more excellent than theirs" (Heb. 1:1–4).

***

"Heart of Jesus, holy temple of God, have mercy on us."

"One thing have I asked of the Lord, that will I seek after;
that I may dwell in the house of the Lord all the day of my life,
to behold the beauty of the Lord, and to inquire in his temple" (Ps. 27:4).

"The Lord is in his holy temple; let all the earth keep silence before him" (Hab. 2:20).

"Jesus answered them, 'Destroy this temple, and in three days I will raise it up'...But he spoke of the temple of his body" (John 2:19, 21).

"And I saw the holy city, new Jerusalem, coming down out of heaven from God, prepared as a bride adorned for her husband…and I saw no temple in the city, for its temple is the Lord God the Almighty and the Lamb" (Rev. 21:2, 22).

***

"Heart of Jesus, tabernacle of the Most High, have mercy on us."

"He will be great, and will be called the Son of the Most High; and the Lord God will give to him the throne of his father David" (Luke 1:32).

***

"Heart of Jesus, house of God and gate of heaven, have mercy on us."

"And he was afraid, and said, 'How awesome is this place! This is none other than the house of God, and this is the gate of heaven'" (Gen. 28:17).

"This is the gate of the Lord; the righteous shall enter through it" (Ps. 118:20).

"And he said to him, 'Truly, truly, I say to you, you will see heaven opened, and the angels of

God ascending and descending upon the Son of man'" (John 1:51).

"I am the door; if anyone enters by me, he will be saved, and will go in and out and find pasture" (John 10:9).

**

"Heart of Jesus, glowing furnace of charity, have mercy on us."

"I will make with them an everlasting covenant, that I will not turn away from doing good to them" (Jer. 32:40).

"Greater love has no man than this, that a man lay down his life for his friends" (John 15:13).

"And there appeared to them tongues as of fire, distributed and resting on each one of them. And they were all filled with the Holy Spirit and began to speak in other tongues, as the Spirit gave them utterance" (Acts 2:3–4).

"Therefore let us be grateful for receiving a kingdom that cannot be shaken, and thus let us offer to God acceptable worship, with reverence and awe, for our God is a consuming fire" (Heb. 12:28–29).

***

"Heart of Jesus, vessel of justice and love, have mercy on us."

"Righteousness and justice are the foundation of his throne" (Ps. 97:2).

"They shall pour forth the fame of thy abundant goodness, and shall sing aloud of thy righteousness" (Ps. 145:7).

"I bring near my deliverance, it is not far off, and my salvation will not tarry;
I will put my salvation in Zion, for Israel is my glory" (Isa. 46:13).

"For God so loved the world that he gave his only Son, that whoever believes in him should not perish but have eternal life" (John 3:16).

"When all things are subjected to him, then the Son himself will also be subjected to him who put all things under him, that God may be everything to every one" (1 Cor. 15:28).

"The life I now live in the flesh I live by faith in the Son of God, who loved me and gave himself for me" (Gal. 2:20).

"Thou has loved righteousness and hated lawlessness" (Heb. 1:9).

"After this I heard what seemed to be the loud voice of a great multitude in heaven, crying, 'Hallelujah! Salvation and glory and power belong to our God, for his judgments are true and just'" (Rev. 19:1–2).

***

"Heart of Jesus, full of goodness and love, have mercy on us."

"Those who are well have no need of a physician, but those who are sick" (Matt. 9:12).

"He loved them to the end" (John 13:1).

"He went about doing good and healing all that were oppressed by the devil, for God was with him" (Acts 10:38).

"Love is patient and kind" (1 Cor. 13:4).

"Beloved, let us love one another; for love is of God, and he who loves is born of God and knows God" (1 John 4:7).

***

"Heart of Jesus, abyss of all virtues, have mercy on us."

"Come to me, you who desire me, and eat your fill of my produce. For the remembrance of me is sweeter than honey, and my inheritance sweeter than the honeycomb" (Sir. 24:18–19).

"Take my yoke upon you, and learn from me; for I am gentle and lowly in heart, and you will find rest for your souls" (Matt. 11:29).

"Every one who thus hopes in him purifies himself as he is pure" (1 John 3:3).

***

"Heart of Jesus, most worthy of all praise, have mercy on us."

"Let all men speak, and give him thanks in Jerusalem" (Tob. 13:8).

"Make a joyful noise to the Lord, all the earth; break forth into joyous song and sing praises" (Ps. 98:4).

"Enter his gates with thanksgiving, and his courts with praise!" (Ps. 100:4).

"Praise God in his sanctuary, praise him in his mighty firmament" (Ps. 150:1).

"Far be it from me to glory except in the cross of our Lord Jesus Christ" (Gal. 6:14).

"And again, when he brings the firstborn into the world, he says, 'Let all God's angels worship him'" (Heb. 1:6).

"They sang a new hymn, saying, 'Worthy art thou to take the scroll and to open its seals, for thou was slain and by thy blood didst ransom men for God from every tribe and tongue and people and nation, and thou hast made them a kingdom and priests to our God, and they shall reign on earth...Worthy is the Lamb who was slain, to receive power and wealth and wisdom and might and honor and glory and blessing'" (Rev. 5:9, 12).

***

"Heart of Jesus, King and center of all hearts, have mercy on us."

"The Lord reigns; let the earth rejoice; let the many coastlands be glad" (Ps. 97:1).

"They shall speak of the glory of thy kingdom, and tell of thy power, to make known to the sons

of men thy mighty deeds, and the glorious splendor of thy kingdom. Thy kingdom is an everlasting kingdom, and thy dominion endures throughout all generations" (Ps. 145:11–13).

"I will give them one heart and one way, that
they may fear me for ever, for their own good and
the good of their children after them" (Jer. 32:39).

"And I will give them one heart, and put a
new spirit within them; I will take the stony heart
out of their flesh and give them a heart of flesh,
that they may walk in my statutes and keep my
ordinances and obey them; and they shall be my
people, and I will be their God" (Ezek. 11:19–20).

"My kingship is not of this world" (John 18:36).

"He has delivered us from the dominion of
darkness and transferred us to the kingdom of his
beloved Son, in whom we have redemption, the
forgiveness of sins" (Col. 1:13–14).

"Thou didst make him for a little while lower
than the angels, thou has crowned him with glory
and honor, putting everything in subjection under
his feet" (Heb. 2:7–8).

"On his robe and on his thigh he has a name
inscribed, King of kings and Lord of lords" (Rev.
19:16).

***

"Heart of Jesus, wherein are all the treasures of wisdom and knowledge, have mercy on us."

"My mouth shall speak wisdom; the meditation of my heart shall be understanding" (Ps. 49:3).

"I thank thee, Father, Lord of heaven and earth, that thou hast hidden these things from the wise and understanding and revealed them to babes" (Matt. 11:25).

"That their hearts may be encouraged as they are knit together in love, to have all the richness of assured understanding and the knowledge of God's mystery, of Christ, in whom are hid all the treasures of wisdom and knowledge" (Col. 2:2–3).

***

"Heart of Jesus, wherein dwells all the fullness of the Godhead, have mercy on us."

"For in him all the fullness of God was pleased to dwell" (Col. 1:19).

"For in him the whole fullness of deity dwells bodily, and you have come to fullness of life in

him, who is the head of all rule and authority"
(Col. 2:9–10).

***

"Heart of Jesus, in whom the Father is well
pleased."

"All things were made through him, and without him was not anything made that was made"
(John 1:3).

"And God saw everything that he had made,
and behold, it was very good" (Gen. 1:31).

"Behold my servant, whom I uphold, my chosen, in whom my soul delights; I have put my
spirit upon him, he will bring forth justice to the
nations" (Isa. 42:1).

"And lo, a voice from heaven, saying, 'This is
my beloved Son, with whom I am well pleased'"
(Matt. 3:17).

"A bright cloud overshadowed them, and a
voice from the cloud said, 'This is my beloved
Son, with whom I am well pleased; listen to him'"
(Matt. 17:5).

***

"Heart of Jesus, of whose fullness we have all received, have mercy on us."

"And I tell you, Ask, and it will be given you; seek, and you will find; knock, and it will be opened to you. For everyone who asks receives, and he who seeks finds, and to him who knocks it will be opened" (Luke 11:9–10).

"And from his fullness have we all received, grace upon grace" (John 1:16).

***

"Heart of Jesus, desire of the everlasting hills, have mercy on us."

"The blessings of your father are mighty beyond the blessings of the eternal mountains, the bounties of the everlasting hills" (Gen. 49:26).

"I lift up my eyes to the hills.
From whence does my help come?
My help comes from the Lord,
who made heaven and earth" (Ps. 121:1–2).

"Sing for joy, O heavens, and exult, O earth;
break forth, O mountains, into singing!
For the Lord has comforted his people,
and will have compassion on his afflicted"
(Isa. 49:13).

***

"Heart of Jesus, patient and rich in mercy, have mercy on us."

"The Lord passed before him, and proclaimed, 'The Lord, the Lord, a God merciful and gracious, slow to anger, and abounding in steadfast love and faithfulness'" (Exod. 34:6).

"I acknowledged my sin to thee,
and I did not hide my iniquity;
I said, 'I will confess my
transgressions to the Lord;
then thou didst forgive the guilt
of my sin'" (Ps. 32:5).

"Let us fall into the hands of the Lord,
but not into the hands of men;
for as his majesty is,
so also is his mercy" (Sir. 2:18).

"Come now, let us reason together,
Says the Lord:
though your sins are like scarlet,
they shall be as white as snow;
though they are red like crimson,
they shall become like wool" (Isa. 1:18).

"Again, though I say to the wicked, 'You shall surely die,' yet if he turns from his sin and does what is lawful and right, if the wicked restores the pledge, gives back what he has taken by robbery, and walks in the statutes of life, committing no iniquity; he shall surely live, he shall not die. None of the sins that he has committed shall be remembered against him; he has done what is lawful and right, he shall surely live" (Ezek. 33:14–16).

"Jesus was left alone with the woman standing before him. Jesus looked up and said to her, 'Woman, where are they? Has no one condemned you?' She said, 'No one, Lord.' And Jesus said, 'Neither do I condemn you; go, and do not sin again'" (John 8:9–11).

"May the Lord direct your hearts to the love of God and to the steadfastness of Christ" (2 Thess. 3:5).

"So let us then with confidence draw near to the throne of grace, that we may receive mercy and find grace to help in time of need" (Heb. 4:16).

***

"Heart of Jesus, rich unto all who call upon you, have mercy on us."

"For thou, O Lord, art good and forgiving,
abounding in steadfast love to all who call on thee" (Ps. 86:5).

"The Lord is near to all who call upon him,
to all who call upon him in truth" (Ps. 145:18).

"Love righteousness, you rulers of the earth,
think of the Lord with uprightness,
and seek him with sincerity of heart;
because he is found by those who do not put
him to the test,
and manifests himself to those who do not
detest him" (Wisd. of Sol. 1:1–2).

"When the wine gave out, the mother of Jesus
said to him, 'They have no wine'" (John 2:3).

"The same Lord is Lord of all and bestows his
riches upon all who call upon him" (Rom. 10:12).

"But if any of you lacks wisdom, let him ask
God, who gives to all men generously and without reproaching, and it will be given him" (James
1:5).

***

"Heart of Jesus, fount of life and holiness, have
mercy on us."

"There is a river whose streams make glad the
city of God,
the holy habitation of the Most High" (Ps.
46:4).

"With joy you will draw water from the wells of salvation" (Isa. 12:3).

"The water that I shall give him will become in him a spring of water welling up to eternal life" (John 4:14).

"Out of his heart shall flow rivers of living water" (John 7:38).

"All drank the same supernatural drink. For they drank from the supernatural Rock which followed them, and the Rock was Christ" (1 Cor. 10:4).

"For the Lamb in the midst of the throne will be their shepherd, and he will guide them to springs of living water...To the thirsty I will give from the fountain of the water of life...Then he showed me the river of the water of life, bright as crystal, flowing from the throne of God and of the Lamb" (Rev. 7:17, 21:6, 22:1).

***

"Heart of Jesus, propitiation for our offenses, have mercy on us."

"He breathed on them, and said to them, 'Receive the Holy Spirit. If you forgive the sins of any, they are forgiven'" (John 20:22–23).

"They are justified by his grace as a gift, through the redemption which is in Christ Jesus, whom God put forward as an expiation by his blood, to be received by faith" (Rom. 3:24–25).

"We know that our old self was crucified with him so that the sinful body might be destroyed, and we might no longer be enslaved to sin" (Rom. 6:6).

"He is the expiation for our sins, and not for ours only but also for the sins of the whole world" (1 John 2:2).

***

"Heart of Jesus, overwhelmed with reproaches, have mercy on us."

"I am poured out like water,
and all my bones are out of joint;
my heart is like wax,
it is melted within my breast" (Ps. 22:14).

"Thou knowest my reproach,
and my shame and my dishonor;
my foes are all known to thee.
Insults have broken my heart,
so that I am in despair.
I looked for pity, but there was none;

and for comforters, but I found none.
They gave me poison for food,
and for my thirst they gave me vinegar to drink" (Ps. 69:19–21).

"As many were astonished at him—
his appearance was so marred,
beyond human semblance...
He was despised and rejected by men;
a man of sorrows, and acquainted with grief" (Isa. 52:14, 53:3).

"Let him give his cheek to the smiter,
And be filled with insults" (Lam. 3:30).

"The Son of Man came eating and drinking, and they say, 'Behold, a glutton and a drunkard, a friend of tax collectors and sinners!'" (Matt. 11:19).

"Now the tax collectors and sinners were all drawing near to hear him. And the Pharisees and the scribes murmured, saying, 'This man receives sinners and eats with them'" (Luke 15:1–2).

"And those who passed by derided him, wagging their heads and saying, 'You who would destroy the temple and build it in three days, save yourself! If you are the Son of God, come down from the cross'" (Matt. 27:40).

***

"Heart of Jesus, bruised for our iniquities, have mercy on us."

"Surely he has borne our griefs and carried our sorrows;
yet we esteemed him stricken, smitten by God, and afflicted.
But he was wounded for our transgressions,
he was bruised for our iniquities;
upon him was the chastisement that made us whole,
and with his stripes we are healed.
All we like sheep have gone astray;
we have turned every one to his own way;
and the Lord has laid on him the iniquity of us all" (Isa. 53:4–6).

"He himself bore our sins in his body on the tree, that we might die to sin and live to righteousness. By his wounds you have been healed" (1 Pet. 2:24).

***

"Heart of Jesus, obedient even unto death, have mercy on us."

"I delight to do thy will, O my God;
thy law is within my heart" (Ps. 40:8).

"And he said to them, 'How is it that you sought me? Did you not know that I must be in my Father's house?'" (Luke 2:49).

"Thy kingdom come.
Thy will be done,
On earth as it is in heaven" (Matt. 6:10).

"My food is to do the will of him who sent me, and to accomplish his work" (John 4:34).

"Father, if thou art willing, remove this cup from me; nevertheless not my will, but thine, be done" (Luke 22:42).

"And being found in human form he humbled himself and became obedient unto death, even death on a cross" (Phil. 2:8).

***

"Heart of Jesus, pierced with a lance, have mercy on us."

"And I will pour out on the house of David and the inhabitants of Jerusalem a spirit of compassion and supplication, so that, when they look on him whom they have pierced, they shall mourn for him, as one mourns for an only child, and weep bitterly over him, as one weeps over a first-born" (Zech. 12:10).

"But one of the soldiers pierced his side with a spear, and at once there came out blood and water" (John 19:34).

"This is he who came by water and blood, Jesus Christ, not with the water only but with the water and the blood" (1 John 5:6).

***

"Heart of Jesus, source of all consolation, have mercy on us."

> "Comfort, comfort my people,
> says your God.
> Speak tenderly to Jerusalem,
> and cry to her
> that her warfare is ended,
> that her iniquity is pardoned" (Isa. 40:1–2).

> "I, I am he that comforts you" (Isa. 51:12).

> "The spirit of the Lord God is upon me,
> because the Lord has anointed me
> to bring good tidings to the afflicted;
> he has sent me to bind up the brokenhearted,
> to proclaim liberty to the captives,
> and the opening of the prison to those who
> are bound;
> to proclaim the year of the Lord's favor,
> and the day of vengeance of our God;

to comfort all who mourn" (Isa. 61:1–2).

"Rejoice with Jerusalem, and be glad for her,
all you who love her;
rejoice with her in joy,
all you who mourn over her;
that you may suck and be satisfied
with her consoling breasts;
that you may drink deeply with delight
from the abundance of her glory.
For thus says the Lord:
Behold, I will extend prosperity to her like a river,
and the wealth of the nations like an overflowing stream;
and you shall suck, you shall be carried upon
her hip and dandled upon her knees.
As one whom his mother comforts,
so I will comfort you;
you shall be comforted in Jerusalem" (Isa.
66:10–13).

"Now there was a man in Jerusalem, whose
name was Simeon, and this man was righteous
and devout, looking for the consolation of Israel,
and the Holy Spirit was upon him" (Luke 2:25).

"Go and tell John what you hear and see: the
blind receive their sight and the lame walk, lepers are cleansed and the deaf hear, and the dead
are raised up, and the poor have good news
preached to them" (Matt. 11:4–5).

"I will not leave you desolate; I will come to you" (John 14:18).

"May the God of steadfastness and encouragement grant you to live in such harmony with one another, in accord with Christ Jesus" (Rom. 15:5).

***

"Heart of Jesus, our life and resurrection, have mercy on us."

"In him was life, and the life was the light of men. The light shines in the darkness, and the darkness has not overcome it" (John 1:4–5).

"I came that they may have life, and have it abundantly" (John 10:10).

"I am the resurrection and the life; he who believes in me, though he die, yet shall he live, and whoever lives and believes in me shall never die" (John 11:25).

"I am the way, and the truth, and the life; no one comes to the Father, but by me" (John 14:6).

"But in fact Christ has been raised from the dead, the first fruits of those who have fallen asleep" (1 Cor. 15:20).

***

"Heart of Jesus, our peace and reconciliation, have mercy on us."

"For to us a child is born,
to us a son is given;
and the government will be upon his shoulder,
and his name will be called
'Wonderful Counselor, Mighty God,
Everlasting Father, Prince of Peace'" (Isa. 9:6).

"Glory to God in the highest,
and on earth peace among men with whom he is pleased!" (Luke 2:14).

"And he said to the woman, 'Your faith has saved you; go in peace'" (Luke 7:50).

"For if while we were enemies we were reconciled to God by the death of his Son, much more, now that we are reconciled, shall we be saved by his life" (Rom. 5:10).

"Have no anxiety about anything, but in everything by prayer and supplication with thanksgiving let your requests be made known to God. And the peace of God, which passes all understanding, will keep your hearts and your minds in Christ Jesus" (Phil. 4:6–7).

"For in him all the fullness of God was pleased to dwell, and through him to reconcile to himself all things, whether on earth or in heaven, making peace by the blood of his cross" (Col. 1:20).

***

"Heart of Jesus, victim for our sins, have mercy on us."

"Then Moses called all the elders of Israel, and said to them, 'Select lambs for yourselves according to your families, and kill the passover lamb'" (Exod. 12:21).

"He was oppressed, and he was afflicted,
yet he opened not his mouth;
like a lamb that is led to the slaughter,
and like a sheep that before its shearers is dumb,
so he opened not his mouth" (Isa. 53:7).

"Behold, the Lamb of God, who takes away the sin of the world!" (John 1:29).

"And he took a cup, and when he had given thanks he gave it to them, saying, 'Drink of it, all of you; for this is my blood of the covenant, which is poured out for many for the forgiveness of sins'" (Matt. 26:27–28).

"For our sake he made him to be sin who knew no sin, so that in him we might become the righteousness of God" (2 Cor. 5:21).

***

"Heart of Jesus, salvation of those who hope in You, have mercy on us."

"The Lord is my strength and my song,
and he has become my salvation" (Exod. 15:2).

"Help us, O God of our salvation
for the glory of thy name;
deliver us, and forgive our sins,
for thy name's sake" (Ps. 79:9).

"I will give you as a light to the nations,
that my salvation may reach to the end of the earth" (Isa. 49:6).

"Lord, now lettest thou thy servant depart in peace,
according to thy word;
for mine eyes have seen the salvation
which thou has prepared in the presence of all peoples,
a light for revelation to the Gentiles,
and for glory to thy people Israel" (Luke 2:29–32).

"For the Son of Man came to seek and to save the lost" (Luke 19:10).

"Every one who calls upon the name of the Lord will be saved" (Rom. 10:13).

"For to this end we toil and strive, because we have our hope set on the living God, who is the savior of all men, especially of those who believe" (1 Tim. 4:10).

"For the grace of God has appeared for the salvation of all men" (Titus 2:11).

***

"Heart of Jesus, hope of those who die in You, have mercy on us."

"Hope in God! For I shall again praise him, my help and my God" (Ps. 42:11).

"Oh send out thy light and thy truth;
let them lead me,
let them bring me to thy holy hill
and to thy dwelling" (Ps. 43:4).

"Truly, truly, I say to you, unless a grain of wheat falls into the earth and dies, it remains alone; but if it dies, it bears much fruit" (John 12:24).

"And when I go and prepare a place for you, I will come again and will take you to myself, that where I am you may be also" (John 14:3).

"But we would not have you ignorant, brethren, concerning those who are asleep, that you may not grieve as others do who have no hope. For since we believe that Jesus died and rose again, even so, through Jesus, God will bring with him those who have fallen asleep" (1 Thess. 4:13–14).

***

"Heart of Jesus, delight of all the saints, have mercy on us."

"Then my soul shall rejoice in the Lord, exulting in his deliverance" (Ps. 35:9).

"Enter into the joy of your master" (Matt. 25:21).

"As the Father has loved me, so have I loved you" (John 15:9).

"And the city has no need of sun or moon to shine upon it, for the glory of God is its light, and its lamp is the Lamb" (Rev. 21:23).

The efficacy of this prayer became apparent in 1720 when a deadly plague struck the city of Marseilles in France, killing some forty thousand people. The bishop and other city leaders consecrated the city to the Sacred Heart, and citizens were asked to join in processions through the streets while reciting litanies and other prayers to the Sacred Heart of Jesus. The Lord responded by stopping the plague immediately. The Litany draws the blessings of heaven down on the earth so dramatically that it is one of the most powerful prayers available to Christians outside of the Mass.

Nine

Reparation to the Sacred Heart

So, could you not watch with me one hour?

Matthew 26:40

Then Jesus, crying with a loud voice, said, "Father, into thy hands I commit my spirit!"

Luke 23:46

I know you are enduring patiently and bearing up for my name's sake, and you have not grown weary. But I have this against you, that you have abandoned the love you had at first. Remember then from what you have fallen, repent and do the works you did at first.

Revelation 2:3–5

One of the primary purposes of the devotion to the Sacred Heart is to give Christians an efficacious means of making reparation to Jesus for our sins. Disciples of Christ are called to offer God some recompense for their sins and, in a spirit of fraternal generosity and charity, for the sins of others as well. Some people hesitate to make amends for the sins of others, believing it is an undertaking reserved only for those who have reached a high degree of sanctity. But God receives all such offerings with joy, because those who make reparation for sin join Jesus in the work of redemption.

Saint Margaret Mary understood that Jesus calls His followers to offer reparation for sin to apply the graces thus gained to everyone. In one letter she noted that this work is directly linked to the Passion.

> There is nothing I would not do or suffer to give Him the pleasure He so ardently desires. And this first of all to re-enkindle love for God, which is burning so low and is almost extinguished in the hearts of most Christians. He wants to give them a new means, by this devotion, of loving God through this Sacred Heart; of loving God as much as He wishes and merits to be

loved, and to make reparation for their ingratitude. This divine Heart is the treasury of heaven from which precious gold has already been given us in many ways to pay off our debts and purchase heaven. It is the last resource of His love which he holds out to us only that we may profit from it. Woe to them that will not or do not make use of it! He wishes that in sanctifying ourselves we glorify this most loving Heart which has suffered more than all the rest of the human nature of Our Lord Jesus Christ. For from the very first moment of the Incarnation, this Sacred Heart was engulfed in a sea of bitterness. It suffered from the very first moment of His existence until His last breath on the cross. Everything this sacred Humanity suffered interiorly during the cruel torments on the cross this divine Heart felt continuously. That is why God wishes It to be honored with special devotion. In this way men give Him as much joy and pleasure by their love and homage as they did bitterness and anguish by the pain they inflicted on Him.

Here we find a marvelous key to loving God. Many Christians have struggled to find a way to love Him as much as we should—with our whole hearts, our whole souls, our whole minds and all our strength. The saint says we can love Him as we should, "loving God as much as He wishes and merits to be loved," through devotion to His Sacred Heart.

We become more aware of the vicious nature of sin and the need for reparation as we draw closer to Jesus. Devotion to the Sacred Heart gradually imbues the disciples of Christ with a horror of sin and a desire to practice some form of expiation for it. This is a natural outgrowth of being closer to God. The old rationalizations and excuses for sin melt before the blazing flames of the Sacred Heart, and the enlightened soul considers the love and tenderness our Savior deserves.

Offering prayers and acts of reparation for sin is an important work in that it honors the Passion of Jesus and draws mercy and graces down on countless souls. God responds generously, even lavishly, to the work of atonement, pouring out treasures of grace on hardened sinners and the repentant alike. This work also helps us to avoid some of the errors of the modern world while we grow in humility. Many people deny the existence of sin; others theorize that while sin may offend God in some way, it does little harm. Such attitudes make a mockery of the Passion, which would have been unnecessary were it not for sin. Pride is often at the root of sin. Reparation helps us to eliminate pride and grow in humility. We admit our sinfulness and take responsibility for making some recompense to Jesus. We offer thanksgiving to the Father for sending His Son to free us from the bondage that leads to eternal death.

Prayer and works of self-denial are among the ways disciples of the Sacred Heart of Jesus offer reparation to God. Keeping a Holy Hour is one approach to atonement. Saint Margaret Mary introduced this practice at the command of Jesus Himself. Jesus repeatedly told her about how He yearned to be loved. He often complained about the ingratitude and contempt of many souls, asking her to try to make up for their coldness. She recounted one of the great revelations of the Sacred Heart, which took place on a first Friday, in her autobiography.

> On one occasion, whilst the Blessed Sacrament was exposed, feeling wholly withdrawn within myself by an extraordinary recollection of all my senses and powers, Jesus Christ, my sweet Master, presented Himself to me, all resplendent with glory, His Five Wounds shining like so many suns. Flames issued from every part of His Sacred

Humanity, especially from His Adorable Bosom, which resembled an open furnace and disclosed to me His most loving and most amiable Heart, which was the living source of these flames. It was then that He made known to me the ineffable marvels of His pure love and showed me to what an excess He had loved men, from whom he received only ingratitude and contempt. "I feel this more," He said, "than all that I suffered during My Passion. If only they would make Me some return for My love, I should think but little of all I have done for them, and would wish, were it possible, to suffer still more. But the sole return they make for all My eagerness to do them good is to reject Me and treat Me with coldness. Do thou at least console me by supplying for their ingratitude, as far as thou art able." On my representing to Him my inability, He replied: "Behold, this will supply for all that is wanting to thee." And at the same time His Divine Heart being opened, there issued from it a flame so ardent that I thought I should be consumed, for I was wholly penetrated with it, and being no longer able to bear it, I besought Him to have pity on my weakness. "I will be thy strength," He said to me, "fear nothing, but be attentive to My voice and to what I shall require of thee that thou mayest be in the requisite dispositions for the accomplishment of My designs. In the first place thou shalt receive Me in Holy Communion as often as obedience will permit thee, whatever mortification or humiliation it may cause thee, which thou must take as a pledge of My love. Thou shalt, moreover, communicate on the First Friday of each month. Every night between Thursday and Friday I will make thee share in the mortal sadness which I was pleased to feel in the Garden of Olives, and this sadness, without thy being able to understand it, shall reduce thee to a kind of agony harder to endure than death itself. And in order to bear Me company in the humble prayer that I then offered to My Father, in the midst of My anguish, thou shalt rise between eleven o'clock and midnight, and remain prostrate with me for an hour, not only to appease the divine anger by begging mercy for sinners, but also to mitigate in some way the bitterness which I felt at that time on finding Myself abandoned by My apostles, which obliged Me to reproach them for not being able to watch one hour with Me. During that hour thou shalt do what I shall teach thee. But listen, My daughter, believe not lightly and trust not every spirit, for Satan is enraged and will seek to deceive thee. Therefore do nothing without the approval of those who guide thee; being thus under the authority of obedience, his efforts against thee will be in vain, for he has no power over the obedient."

Saint Margaret Mary began keeping the Holy Hour on Thursday nights between 11:00 p.m. and midnight after she received permission from her superior to do so. Many other disciples of the Sacred Heart have followed this practice and variations of it. Some people keep a Holy Hour every week, while others do so monthly on the evening preceding the first Friday of the month. In some parishes a Holy Hour is kept on first Fridays or first Saturdays. Where possible, it is best to spend this hour before the Blessed Sacrament, but it can also be spent at home or in other locations. Many people who observe the Holy Hour do so on Thursdays in the afternoon or evening; it can be kept alone or in a group. Those who keep the hour as a group can find an excellent collection of prayers and meditations in *Twenty Holy Hours* by Father Mateo Crawley-Boevey. The author of this book traveled all over the world to spread devotion to the Sacred Heart of Jesus. He became one of the greatest apostles of the devotion in the twentieth century.

The Holy Hour may be spent in spontaneous prayers of atonement or in a combination of spontaneous and formal prayers. Many different prayers are fitting, including the Litany of the Sacred Heart, the Sorrowful Mysteries of the Rosary, the Way of the Cross, and the Chaplet of Divine Mercy. Part of the hour can be spent reading one of the accounts of the Passion found in the Gospels. This time is most valuable when we join ourselves in spirit to Jesus as He endured the agony in the garden at Gethsemane. Jesus once described His experience there to Saint Margaret Mary with these words:

"Here I suffered more than in the rest of My Passion. I saw Myself wholly abandoned by heaven and earth, and loaded with the burden of the sins of all men. I appeared before the holiness of God who, without considering my innocence, crushed Me in His wrath, causing Me to drink the chalice which was filled with all the bitterness of His righteous anger. The name of Father He seemed to have forgotten, in order to sacrifice

me to His just wrath. No creature is able to understand the violence of the torments which I then
endured."

Atonement for sin acts as a balm for the
wounds Christ suffered for our offenses. We console Him as we would console any suffering friend.
As we grow closer to Jesus, we want to caress
Him with our prayers and anoint His wounds with
our love. This work of atonement also allows us
to break through the barriers of space and time
that restrict most human endeavors. Sins committed in our day afflicted Jesus at Gethsemane and
Calvary, and our works of reparation consoled
Him even though they had not yet taken place.
Just as an angel appeared to Jesus to strengthen
Him during the agony in the garden, our future
reparation also provided Him with great consolation. Perhaps the angel was delivering our future
prayers across time.

Saint Gertrude once experienced a vision in
which Jesus showed her that it is important to
pray and make reparation for our enemies, just as
He did during His Passion. The saint was praying
for some people who had pillaged her community
when Jesus appeared to her. She could see that
His arm was hurt; it looked dislocated and almost
paralyzed. Jesus told her to consider the pain He
would experience if someone were to strike His
dislocated arm with a fist. He said He experienced
such pain when people failed to consider the terrible dangers to which the souls of their persecutors

were exposed. Many people instead recounted the sins of their enemies and the losses they had experienced at their enemies' hands. Jesus told her that such people failed to remember that their enemies were members of His body. He explained that people who prayed for their attackers and regarded them with loving compassion were like those who put a soothing ointment on His injured arm. Jesus also said that those who advised the attackers to change their ways were like skilled doctors who restored His arm to health. He said He had tremendous love for the people who had attacked her community, and He longed for their repentance and conversion.

Our prayers of reparation gain merit before the Father when we offer them through the Heart of Jesus and in union with His sorrowful Passion. By joining ourselves to the sufferings of Gethsemane and Calvary, we share in the redemptive work that is so important to preserving the health of the Mystical Body of Christ.

Some other practices also serve as a means of reparation. For example, acts of self-denial such as fasting can be offered to the Sacred Heart of Jesus. Many of the early Christians fasted regularly on Wednesdays and Fridays, taking only bread for each meal on those days. This practice and variations of it are gaining renewed popularity among contemporary Christians.

We can also make reparation for sin by joining our pains, whatever they may be, to the anguish

Jesus suffered during His Passion. Everyone suffers some pain in life, and many people endure extraordinary trials of body and soul. Suffering is largely an empty, meaningless experience for many souls. However, disciples of the Sacred Heart can offer everything from small annoyances to terrible trials in honor of the Passion, transforming their sorrows into occasions of grace. Saint Margaret Mary wrote that everyone should embrace such unavoidable suffering to become more like Jesus. "The cross is good at all times and in all places. It matters little of what wood it is made, provided that it is offered to us by the Sacred Heart of our Lord."

Certain sacraments also provide opportunities to make reparation for our sins. Confession involves admitting to, and taking responsibility for, our failures and entails a penance as well. In an age that often denies the existence of sin or even the existence of God, this sacrament has become radically countercultural. Confession acknowledges both our capacity for failure and God's infinite mercy.

Offering our Masses and Communions in atonement for sins is also a worthwhile practice. The Mass is a perfect prayer in which Jesus Himself renews the eternal sacrifice of Calvary. Indeed, the Mass has restrained God's wrath against sinners for centuries. The Old Testament is full of examples of God overwhelming sinners with harsh and bitter punishments for their offenses.

Such sweeping chastisements have become less common since Jesus celebrated the first Mass at the Last Supper. The Father sees Jesus descending on the altars and dwelling in the tabernacles of the world. This presence delays the final hour of justice until the full measure of the merciful Heart of Jesus has been poured out on humanity. Offering our Masses with an intention of making reparation for sin is an effective way to draw on the boundless treasures of the Sacred Heart of Jesus. These graces become available to us, members of our families and even strangers as this fountain of mercy strengthens the fervent and offers opportunities for true repentance to all sinners.

We can also offer our Communions for this intention, begging Jesus to have mercy on us and on all who are in need of His forgiveness. Jesus dwells within us and among us when we receive Communion. We can join our prayers to those of His Sacred Heart as we ask the Father to forgive our sins and those of the whole world. The sins of the human race are great in number and severity. Yet we offer the Father something that is infinitely greater: the Sacred Heart of His Son, pulsating with a passionate desire to bring all of humanity to heaven. These Masses and Communions of reparation can be offered on any day of the week and as often as one likes. Disciples of the Sacred Heart make a particular effort to do this on the first Friday of the month. Beyond that, the annual

Feast of the Sacred Heart of Jesus is intended to be a day of reparation for all Catholics.

The present Feast of the Sacred Heart originated with a request from Jesus to Saint Margaret Mary that a special day be set aside to make reparation for sins. This great revelation took place as the saint was in prayer before the Blessed Sacrament. Jesus made this request in 1675. Margaret Mary became a proponent of establishing the feast within the church, but this work didn't become a reality until many years after her death. In 1765 Pope Clement XIII granted observance of the feast to any diocese that requested it. He also approved a special Mass and Office for the feast. He acted at the request of the bishops of Poland. They had mounted an intensive campaign to win official approval of a feast that laypeople and religious alike were already observing unofficially throughout the world. Pope Pius IX extended the feast to the universal church in 1856.

Many disciples of the Sacred Heart also make an effort to intensify their works of reparation during the month of June. The practice of setting aside June as a month dedicated to the Sacred Heart (just as May is dedicated to the Blessed Virgin Mary) originated in nineteenth-century Paris. Pope Leo XIII recommended this practice to the universal church in 1899. June is an opportunity to thank Jesus for all the blessings that have flowed from His pierced Heart throughout the centuries. We can also make some recompense for the sins and ingratitude of humanity.

While practices such as prayer and fasting are acts of spiritual reparation, disciples of the Sacred Heart are also called to engage in social reparation. Saint James' Epistle says that faith without works is dead, just as the body without the spirit is dead. And the passage from the book of Revelation that appears at the beginning of this chapter calls us to "repent, and do the works you did at first." Repentance should lead to good works and is inextricably associated with action. Social reparation involves relieving the suffering caused by individual and societal sins, and working to eliminate social and economic injustice.

One guide to how social reparation operates is the life of Saint Margaret Mary. In her autobiography she said that when she was a teenager, she yearned to become closer to Jesus and asked for His direction.

> I therefore asked Him to teach me and to show me what He wished me to do in order to please Him. This He did in the following manner: He inspired me with so tender a love for the poor that I would gladly have conversed with no other persons. He also impressed upon me such deep feelings of compassion for their miseries that, had it been

in my power, I would have retained nothing for myself; therefore when I had any money, I gave it to poor children to induce them to come to me, that I might teach them their Catechism and their prayers. The consequence was that they flocked round me in such numbers that I knew not where to assemble them in winter time except in a large room, from which we were sometimes driven out. This was a source of great mortification to me, for I did not wish anyone to know what I was about. It was generally thought that I gave to the poor everything that I could find, but I would not have dared do that for fear of taking what did not belong to me; I was careful to give only what was my own, and even that I did not dare do without leave. Indeed, I was obliged to use endearing words to induce my mother to allow me to give away what I had, but, as she loved me tenderly, she consented more or less willingly.

Many people have unlimited opportunities to engage in social reparation. We can give of our time and money to feed the hungry, shelter the homeless, welcome refugees and other immigrants, clothe the poor and care for the sick. A diabolical wave of violence has swept through the world during the past century. We can work to relieve the suffering of victims of war and all other forms of violence. Beyond that we can also work to reform economic systems that exploit people and perpetuate poverty, and we have opportunities to change laws that allow violence or oppression of the poor, aliens or minorities. Similarly, we can work to eliminate crimes against life such as abortion, war and capital punishment.

The task of social reparation can appear to be overwhelming, but Jesus doesn't ask us to repair all the problems of humanity simultaneously. The inspirations of the Holy Spirit bless the disciples of the Sacred Heart. God will suggest ways in which we can serve Him and His people if we ask Him to do so. He can lead our thoughts in such a way that His will for us becomes clear. The inspirations of the Holy Spirit can come in infinite ways and at any time. They come as we read the Bible or hear it read during Mass, during a conversation or while we are in prayer before the Blessed Sacrament or elsewhere. And they can come while we are taking a shower or going for a walk.

In the first chapter of Luke, we find an account of how Mary visited her cousin, Elizabeth. When Mary greeted her, Elizabeth felt her child leap in her womb, and she was filled with the Holy Spirit. Many Christians have had similar experiences, feeling a sudden inner affirmation or surge of energy when the Holy Spirit inspired them to take a certain course of action. This is one way to discern the desires of the Holy Spirit. Anyone who has a sincere desire to engage in the work of social reparation and asks for the guidance of the Holy Spirit will receive it. These inspirations will be a guide to which particular kinds of activity God most wants us to undertake.

Ten

Scriptural Foundations

Thou art God, and thy words are true.

2 Samuel 7:28

Everyone who is of the truth hears my voice.

John 18:37

And he said to them, "O foolish men, and slow of heart to believe all that the prophets have spoken! Was it not necessary that the Christ should suffer these things and enter into his glory?" And beginning with Moses and all the prophets, he interpreted to them in all the scriptures the things concerning himself.

Luke 24:25–27

Many disciples of the Sacred Heart form the habit of reading scripture every day. Perhaps the most common practice is to follow the readings for daily Mass. This helps us to follow the rhythm of the liturgical year and provides us with a reading from one of the Gospels every day. The essence of the Sacred Heart devotion involves learning to live out the Gospels in our daily lives, and every passage of the Gospels reveals the sentiments of Christ's Heart. Through daily exposure to the Gospels, we focus on God and on our own hearts in relationship to Him and all of humanity. We receive encouragement and light, blessing and hope. Through prayerful consideration of God's revelation to us, we discover areas of sin and weakness that are in need of correction and receive the graces we need to change. In time, through prayer and perseverance, we learn to surrender more and more of our lives to Jesus. Our hearts, once hardened, are freed to become truly human hearts.

While the Gospels reveal the Heart of Jesus in a unique way, many passages throughout the Bible have played an important role in the development of the Sacred Heart devotion. God's merciful love is the source of this devotion, and scripture is replete with information about God's love for His people. The Bible contains many references to the Heart of God, some of which speak specifically of the Savior's Heart. The word *heart* appears more than one thousand times in the Bible. Some of these references are to God's own Heart, and many others refer to the hearts of His people.

Every reference to God's Heart reveals something about His relationship with His people. While the Bible sometimes speaks of the human heart considered in itself, many more references to the heart deal with the relationship between people and God. Sometimes the word *heart* is used in the Bible in a clinical sense, referring solely to the heart as an organ, but usually the word has a much deeper and more poetic significance. Heart typically refers to the innermost core, the true essence of a person, a situation or God.

Often Old Testament passages need to be viewed in light of related New Testament texts and vice versa to gain a broad scriptural perspective on the Savior's Heart. Old Testament references to the Heart of God provide important insights into the Sacred Heart of Jesus. While the mystery of the Trinity had not yet been revealed, the ideas expressed in the Hebrew Bible about God's Heart reflect the deepest desires and feelings of all three Persons of the Trinity.

References to God's Heart occur as early as Genesis. In Genesis, after the creation and the fall, God is sorrowful because of the sinfulness He finds among His people. "The Lord saw that the wickedness of man was great in the earth, and that every imagination of the thoughts of his heart was only evil continually. And the Lord was sorry that he had made man on the earth, and it grieved him to his heart" (Gen. 6:5–6).

Here we find intense alienation between God and the human race. This passage occurs just before the story of the flood, which would punish sinners and cleanse the earth, leaving only Noah and his companions alive. But true reconciliation between God and His people wouldn't be accomplished until Jesus died on the cross and until the sanctifying flood of graces from His pierced Heart began to cleanse all who bathed in the waters of baptism and strengthen all who consumed the Eucharist.

Many other Old Testament books also provide some glimpses into the Heart of the Creator. For example, in Samuel we find that God was displeased with Eli because he had been negligent in his priestly duties. God spoke to Eli through a holy man. "And I will raise up for myself a faithful priest, who shall do according to what is in my heart and in my mind; and I will build him a sure house, and he shall go in and out before my anointed forever" (1 Sam. 2:35).

This is one of several Old Testament passages where God said His Heart's desire was to give His people holy leaders by replacing those who displeased Him. In another example Samuel told Saul that Saul's leadership was inadequate and that he would be replaced. "The Lord has sought out a man after his own heart; and the Lord has appointed him to be prince over the people, because you have not kept what the Lord commanded you" (1 Sam. 13:14).

A similar passage occurs in Jeremiah, where God spoke through the prophet. "And I will give you shepherds after my own heart, who will feed you with knowledge and understanding" (Jer. 3:15).

All of these passages show God's concern for His people and His desire to give them good leaders, who were forerunners of the special relationship between the Sacred Heart of Jesus and the priesthood. God replaced bad priests and leaders with righteous leaders, such as Samuel and David; and ultimately God sent His own Son, the Good Shepherd, who would lead His flock to the Father.

The prophet Nathan told David of the promise of a holy leader, the Messiah Himself, after David proposed building a house for God to dwell in. God spoke through Nathan, saying that He would establish a house and a kingdom for David that would endure forever, and the Messiah who would do this work would be among David's descendants. David responded with joy and offered a humble prayer of thanksgiving to God. "Because of thy promise, and according to thy own heart, thou has wrought all this greatness, to make thy servant know it" (2 Sam. 7:21).

David saw the promise of a Messiah, an act of incomparable generosity, as coming from the very Heart of God. Centuries later the Heart of the Messiah would become the source of salvation for the human race.

David's son, Solomon, had the honor of building God's temple in Jerusalem. Solomon offered a prayer, asking God to consecrate the temple, and God appeared to Solomon and spoke to him.

"And the Lord said to him, 'I have heard your prayer and your supplication, which you have made before me; I have consecrated this house which you have built, and put my name there for ever; my eyes and my heart will be there for all time'" (1 Kings 9:3).

Here we see God's Heart expanding to give His attentive and loving presence to His people as a permanent gift. They would have a place to go where their prayers would be heard; indeed, God sanctified the temple by making it His own dwelling place. The institution of the Eucharist at the Last Supper was a similar act in which Jesus made a commitment to dwell with His people by making Himself present on altars, in tabernacles and within His disciples until the end of time.

The wisdom books also contain references to God's Heart. In the book of Job, for example, Job spoke of God's wisdom and omnipotence. "He is wise in heart and mighty in strength—who has hardened himself against him, and succeeded?" (Job 9:4).

Devotion to the Sacred Heart involves making a commitment to do just the opposite of withstanding God. Jesus once described His guidance of souls to Saint Margaret Mary as both wise and fruitful. "I will make thee understand that I am a wise and learned director, who will safely lead those souls who, forgetful of themselves, abandon themselves to Me."

The Book of Psalms is one of the richest sources of revelation about the Heart of God in the Old Testament. Some psalms are, in whole or in part, prophecies about Jesus; these are the Messianic Psalms. For example, in one passage we find a prophetic statement about the Heart of Jesus rejoicing in the victory over sin and death that would be won for the human race.

> Therefore my heart is glad, and my soul rejoices;
> my body also dwells secure.
> For thou dost not give me up to Sheol,
> or let thy godly one see the Pit.
> Thou dost show me the path of life;
> in thy presence there is fullness of joy,
> in thy right hand are pleasures for evermore. (Ps. 16:9–11)

Both Saint Paul and Saint Peter affirmed that this passage was a prophecy about the resurrection of Jesus rather than a statement about David, who is credited with writing many of the psalms.

Their testimony about this appears in the Acts of the Apostles. Saint Paul, in a speech recorded in Acts, said this was among several psalms that refer to the Messiah (Acts 13:32–37).

Saint Peter, in his great speech to the crowd gathered after the descent of the Holy Spirit at Pentecost, quoted the psalm and then gave this interpretation: "Brethren, I may say to you confidently of the patriarch David that he both died and was buried, and his tomb is with us to this day. Being therefore a prophet, and knowing that God had sworn with an oath to him that he would set one of his descendants upon his throne, he foresaw and spoke of the resurrection of the Christ, that he was not abandoned to Hades, nor did his flesh see corruption. This Jesus God raised up, and of that we all are witnesses" (Acts 2:29–32).

And so we find the Heart of Jesus at the center of the extraordinary events of Pentecost as the Holy Spirit gave birth to the Church. The Sacred Heart expresses ineffable joy in the psalm, and Jesus shared this joy with His disciples through a tremendous outpouring of the Holy Spirit.

While Psalm 16 speaks of joy, Psalm 22 reveals the suffering wrought in the Heart of Christ during His Passion. The psalm begins with the haunting cry of abandonment Jesus uttered on the cross. "My God, my God, why hast thou forsaken me?" (Ps. 22:1; Matt. 27:46).

The psalm continues and tells of how the Heart of Jesus, aflame with love for humanity, would melt during the Passion, consuming itself in a selfless act of obedience to the Father's will.

> I am poured out like water,
> and all my bones are out of joint;
> my heart is like wax,
> it is melted within my breast;
> my strength is dried up like a potsherd,
> and my tongue cleaves to my jaws;
> thou dost lay me in the dust of death.
> Yea, dogs are round about me; a company of evildoers encircle me;
> they have pierced my hands and feet—
> I can count all my bones—
> they stare and gloat over me;
> they divide my garments among them,
> and for my raiment they cast lots.
> (Ps. 22:14–18)

Several New Testament passages (as well as Matt. 27:46) confirm that this psalm is a prophecy about the crucifixion. "And when they had crucified him, they divided his garments among them by casting lots" (Matt. 27:35).

John's Gospel is clear about the relationship between this psalm and the Crucifixion; it states that the casting of lots is a fulfillment of the prophecy in this psalm (John 19:23–24).

Psalm 69 is also a prophecy about the Passion that describes the terrible suffering the Heart of Jesus endured:

Insults have broken my heart,
so that I am in despair.
I looked for pity, but there was none;
and for comforters, but I found none.
They gave me poison for food,
and for my thirst they gave me vinegar
to drink. (Ps. 69:20–21)

Here we find the Heart of Jesus in anguish as He suffered on the cross, surrounded by tormentors who offered Him nothing but a bitter drink to quench His thirst. Several New Testament passages confirm that this psalm is about Jesus, and one part of the psalm is a prophecy about the cleansing of the Temple.

> For zeal for thy house has consumed me,
> and the insults of those who insult thee have fallen on me. (Ps. 69:9)

John's account of the cleansing of the temple refers directly to this psalm (John 2:14–17). Saint

Paul referred to the same verse of the psalm to describe Jesus and urged Christians to live together in harmony (Rom. 15:1–6).

Another verse of the psalm refers to the hatred directed against Jesus.

More in number than the hairs of my head are those who hate me without cause" (Ps. 69:4).

At the Last Supper, Jesus told His disciples that the hatred directed against Him was in fulfillment of this psalm. "If I had not done among them the works which no one else did, they would not have sin; but now they have seen and hated both me and my Father. It is to fulfil the word that is written in their law, 'They have hated me without a cause'" (John 15:24–25).

Another verse of the psalm is about the final fate of Judas. "May their camp be a desolation, let no one dwell in their tents" (Ps. 69:25).

Saint Peter (in Acts 1:16–20) said this encampment is a reference to the plot of land purchased with the money Judas received for betraying Jesus; the plot came to be known as the "Field of Blood."

This psalm and the New Testament passages associated with it contain many of the themes associated with devotion to the Sacred Heart throughout the ages. We find compassion for the brokenhearted Savior who suffered unspeakable trials during His Passion, the ingratitude of some of His disciples, the hatred directed against Him and His disciples and His zeal for bringing people into a pure relationship with the Father.

Psalm 33 offers another perspective on God's
Heart, portraying it as steadfast and unchanging
in a world where many things are in flux, and the
plans of people often don't work out because
they are opposed to God's will.

> The Lord brings the counsel of the
> nations to nought;
> he frustrates the plans of the
> peoples.
> The counsel of the Lord stands for
> ever,
> the thoughts of his heart to all gen-
> erations. (Ps. 33:10–11)

When Jesus revealed Himself and the designs
of His Heart to Saint Margaret Mary, He often
described His Sacred Heart as an infinitely peaceful refuge where people could seek shelter from
the storms of life—especially a refuge for sinners
who would otherwise face harsh punishment for
their transgressions.

Psalm 40 also contains a reference to the
Heart of the Messiah, a Heart that delights in
obedience to the will of the Father.

> Sacrifice and offering thou dost not
> desire;
> but thou hast given me an open ear.
> Burnt offering and sin offering thou
> has not required.

Then I said, "Lo, I come;
in the roll of the book it is written of me;
I delight to do thy will, O my God;
thy law is within my heart." (Ps. 40:6–8)

The author of the Epistle to the Hebrews quoted this psalm, saying it refers to Jesus and then explained that the sacrifice of His body was the only sacrifice that could take away the sins of the world.

The prophets also provided some insights into the Heart of God. Jeremiah mentioned God's Heart several times. God spoke through Jeremiah to express His intense anger at false prophets who had led Israel astray by failing to condemn sin and by telling people that they could sin without fear of punishment. Jeremiah told of the Babylonian Captivity, a period of death and destruction for God's people, which would come about because of sin. God revealed Himself as a passionate, jealous lover who longed to be one with His people. The punishment for their sins was a manifestation of His love; He was willing to go to any lengths to bring His people back to Him. Yet even in His anger, which led Him to allow vicious enemies to overwhelm Jerusalem and carry His people off to Babylon, God made plans to free them and pour out His blessings on them.

And they shall be my people,
and I will be their God. I will give
them one heart and one way, that

they may fear me for ever, for their own good and the good of their children after them. I will make with them an everlasting covenant, that I will not turn away from doing good to them; and I will put the fear of me in their hearts, that they may not turn from me. I will rejoice in doing them good, and I will plant them in this land in faithfulness, with all my heart and all my soul. (Jer. 32:38–41)

A similar passage occurs in Hosea, where God affirms His love for the people who have wandered so far from Him and declares that their suffering and exile will end. Here we see God's merciful love overcoming His anger.

> My heart recoils within me,
> my compassion grows warm and tender.
> I will not execute my fierce anger. (Hosea 11:8–9)

The Old Testament, with its many references to God's Heart, established many of the themes that would emerge in later revelations about the Sacred Heart of Jesus. Some New Testament passages also provide specific insights into the Savior's Heart.

Several texts from the Gospels of Matthew and John have been important in the development of the Sacred Heart devotion. We find Jesus revealing His Heart when He spoke of His unique relationship with the Father and issued an invitation to discipleship.

> At that time Jesus declared, "I thank thee, Father, Lord of heaven and earth, that thou has hidden these things from the wise and understanding and revealed them to babes; yea, Father, for such was thy gracious will. All things have been delivered to me by my Father; and no one knows the Son except the Father, and no one knows the Father except the Son and any one to whom the Son chooses to reveal him. Come to me, all who labor and are heavy laden, and I will give you rest. Take my yoke upon you, and learn from me; for I am gentle and lowly in heart, and you will find rest for your souls. For my yoke is easy, and my burden is light." (Matt. 11:25–30)

Here we find Jesus declaring that the Father handed all things over to Him, followed by an invitation to discipleship that involves learning from Jesus, who is "gentle and lowly in heart." The Heart of Jesus is presented as the source of all blessings. Jesus revealed the Father to His disciples through the enlightenment of the Holy Spirit; the Sacred Heart became the opening or entry point into the inner life of the Holy Trinity, the place of refuge and rest, the way to knowledge of God and eternal life. We are to come to Jesus because His Heart provides an efficacious way to enter into the abundant graces and infinite mystery of the Trinity. The Trinitarian nature of this invitation to discipleship is highlighted in Luke's description of this discourse (Luke 10:21–22), which describes Jesus as rejoicing in the Spirit as He says these words.

The wording of this passage from Matthew is strikingly similar to several Old Testament passages about wisdom. The linguistic likenesses suggest that the Heart of Jesus is the source of true wisdom for the human race. In the Old Testament, wisdom is often personified (presented as Wisdom, not wisdom), and referred to as "she." For example, in Proverbs we find Wisdom giving a discourse.

> And now, my sons, listen to me:
> happy are those who keep my ways.
> Hear instruction and be wise,
> and do not neglect it.

Happy is the man who listens to
me,
Watching daily at my gates,
waiting beside my doors.
For he who finds me finds life
and obtains favor from the Lord;
but he who misses me injures
himself;
all who hate me love death.
(Prov. 8:32–36)

A similar passage is found in the book of
Wisdom, where Solomon addressed a prayer to
God.

For the reasoning of mortals is
worthless,
and our designs are likely to fail,
for a perishable body weighs
down the soul,
and the earthy tent burdens the
thoughtful mind.
We can hardly guess at what is
on earth,
and what is at hand we find with
labor;
but who has traced out what is
in the heavens?
Who has learned thy counsel,
unless thou hast given wisdom

and sent thy holy Spirit from on
high?
And thus the paths of those on
earth were set right,
and men were taught what
pleases thee,
and were saved by wisdom.
(Wisd. of Sol. 9:14–18)

Several texts from the book of Sirach, when read
in the light of the above discourse in Matthew, also
reveal that God's saving wisdom is embodied in
Jesus. For instance, the following passage speaks
of the blessings of wisdom and bears a remarkable
likeness to the Matthew discourse:

Listen, my son, and accept my
judgment;
do not reject my counsel.
Put your feet into her fetters,
and your neck into her collar.
Put your shoulder under her and
carry her,
and do not fret under her bonds.
Come to her with all your soul,
and keep her ways with all your
might.
Search out and seek, and she
will become known to you;
and when you get hold of her,
do not let her go.

For at last you will find the rest
she gives,
and she will be changed into joy
for you.
Then her fetters will become for
you a strong protection,
and her collar a glorious robe.
Her yoke is a golden ornament,
and her bonds are a cord of
blue.
You will wear her like a glorious
robe,
and put her on like a crown of
gladness. (Sir. 6:23–31)

A similar passage occurs in the last chapter of
the book of Sirach.

Draw near to me, you who are
untaught,
and lodge in my school.
Why do you say you are lacking
in these things,
and why are your souls very
thirsty?
I opened my mouth and said,
Get these things for yourselves
without money.
Put your neck under the yoke,
and let your souls receive
instruction;

it is to be found close by.
See with your eyes that I have
labored little
and found for myself much rest.
(Sir. 51:23–27)

Saint Paul also described Jesus as God's wisdom, confusing the proud and the powerful because of His meekness and gentleness. Jesus transformed a bloody and terrifying death on the cross into the source of salvation and set a pattern His disciples would follow.

"God chose what is foolish in the world to shame the wise, God chose what is weak in the world to shame the strong, God chose what is low and despised in the world, even things that are not, to bring to nothing things that are, so that no human being might boast in the presence of God. He is the source of your life in Christ Jesus, whom God made our wisdom, our righteousness and sanctification and redemption; therefore, as it is written, 'Let him who boasts, boasts of the Lord'" (1 Cor. 1:27–31).

Taken as a whole, these passages present the Heart of Jesus as the house of instruction, the seat of God's wisdom, the place where disciples are called to take up their residence and enter fully into the life of the Holy Trinity. Taking on the easy yoke the Heart of Jesus offers and becoming obedient to Him is the way to eternal life. Jesus is Wisdom Incarnate, the Word made flesh. The

Heart of the Savior is a place of sweetness and rest where we can learn the ways of God.

Note that the phrase "come to me," which is found in the above discourse in Matthew, appears in a slightly different form in John's Gospel, where Jesus spoke of the Eucharist. The linguistic parallels suggest the intimate relationship between the Sacred Heart of Jesus and the Eucharist. "Jesus said to them, 'I am the bread of life; he who comes to me shall not hunger, and he who believes in me shall never thirst'" (John 6:35).

In the next chapter of John's Gospel, we find Jesus in Jerusalem, where He was teaching in the temple area and observing the Feast of Tabernacles. This popular feast commemorates the years of wandering in the desert and serves as a harvest festival in which participants thank God for the rain that led to a plentiful harvest and ask Him for continued rain that will lead to a rich harvest the following year. On the last day of the seven-day feast, a great procession led by the high priest went to the Pool of Siloam. The priest filled a golden urn with water from the pool and led the procession to the Temple, where he poured the water on the sacrificial altar. As he poured the water, the people recited the words of the prophet Isaiah. "With joy you will draw water from the wells of salvation" (Isa. 12:3).

It was on this day that Jesus revealed His Heart as the fountain of salvation.

On the last day of the feast, the great day, Jesus stood up and proclaimed, "If any one thirst, let him come to me and drink. He who believes in me, as the scripture has said, 'Out of his heart shall flow rivers of living water.'" Now this he said about the Spirit, which those who believed in him were to receive; for as yet the Spirit had not been given, because Jesus was not yet glorified (John 7:37–39).

Translators have presented these verses in different ways, with some following a style of punctuation that has rivers of living water flowing out of Jesus, while others have them flowing out of the believer. In either case Jesus is the crowning source of the living water. This passage and the many scriptures related to it played a significant role in drawing attention to the Heart of Jesus in the early Christian church, and we will examine it in some detail.

The Hebrew Bible already established a firm relationship between God's blessings and water because water is so precious to desert dwellers. But the Old Testament also repeatedly identifies water with the Messiah and God's Spirit as well. Some examples of this can help to put the words of Jesus in context.

In Psalm 36 human wickedness is contrasted with divine providence.

> How precious is thy steadfast love,
> O God!

The children of men take refuge in
the shadow of thy wings.
They feast on the abundance of thy
house,
and thou givest them drink from the
river of thy delights.
For with thee is the fountain of life;
in thy light do we see light. (Ps.
36:7–9)

Similarly, Psalm 78 recalls the wonders God
performed for His people when they were lost in
the desert.

He made streams come out of the rock,
And caused water to flow down like
rivers. (Ps. 78:16)

The prophets were full of references to God's
gift of life-giving waters. Isaiah used this imagery
extensively to describe the glory of the Messiah
and the gift of His Spirit.

They shall not hurt or destroy in all
my holy mountain;
for the earth shall be full of the
knowledge of the Lord as the waters
cover the sea. (Isa. 11:9)

Later, Isaiah spoke of Israel's deliverance:

> Then the eyes of the blind will be
> opened,
> and the ears of the deaf unstopped;
> then shall the lame man leap like a hart,
> and the tongue of the dumb sing for joy.
> For waters shall break forth in the
> wilderness,
> and streams in the desert;
> the burning sand shall become a pool,
> and the thirsty ground springs of
> water. (Isa. 35:5–7)

In another passage God spoke through Isaiah to describe Israel's liberation.

> When the poor and needy seek water,
> and there is none,
> and their tongue is parched with
> thirst,
> I the Lord will answer them,
> I the God of Israel will not forsake
> them.
> I will open rivers on the bare heights,
> and fountains in the midst of the
> valleys;
> I will make the wilderness a pool of
> water,
> and the dry land springs of water. (Isa.
> 41:17–18)

God spoke through Isaiah in a similar passage related to the redemption of Israel, making the connection between water and God's own Spirit more direct.

> For I will pour water on the thirsty
> land,
> and streams on the dry ground;
> I will pour my spirit upon your
> descendants,
> and my blessing on your offspring.
> (Isa. 44:3)

And in a passage that is similar to the above invitations from Jesus in Matthew and John, we find this line:

> Ho, every one who thirsts,
> come to the waters. (Isa. 55:1)

Isaiah was not alone among the prophets in using water imagery to paint a portrait of God's blessings. For example, we find God speaking through Jeremiah to describe how God's people had turned away from Him.

> Be appalled, O heavens, at this,
> be shocked, be utterly desolate,
> says the Lord,

for my people have committed two
evils:
they have forsaken me,
the fountain of living waters,
and hewed out cisterns for
themselves,
broken cisterns, that can hold no
water. (Jer. 2:12–13)

Similarly, we find a description of how God
will bring about the regeneration of his people
through water and His Spirit in this passage,
where God speaks through the prophet Ezekiel.
"I will sprinkle clean water upon you, and you
shall be clean from all your uncleannesses, and
from all your idols I will cleanse you. A new heart
will I give you, and a new spirit I will put within
you; and I will take out of your flesh the heart
of stone and give you a heart of flesh. And I will
put my spirit within you, and cause you to walk in
my statutes and be careful to observe my ordinances" (Ezek. 36:25–27).

While the Old Testament describes the
Messiah as the source of a fountain of life-giving
waters associated with God's Spirit, Jesus also
described Himself in those terms in His conversation with the Samaritan woman at the well.

"Jesus said to her, 'Every one who drinks of
this water will thirst again, but whoever drinks of
the water that I shall give him will never thirst; the
water that I shall give him will become in him a

spring of water welling up to eternal life'" (John 4:13–14).

Saint Paul employed this imagery as well in a letter to the Christian community at Corinth, in which he described Israel's period of wandering in the desert. "All ate the same supernatural food and all drank the same supernatural drink. For they drank from the supernatural Rock which followed them, and the Rock was Christ" (1 Cor. 10:3–4).

In the Book of Revelation, God uses similar words after He destroys death and creates a new heaven and a new earth. "I am the Alpha and the Omega, the beginning and the end. To the thirsty I will give from the fountain of the water of life without payment" (Rev. 21:6).

Then God creates a New Jerusalem, and the springs of water appear. "Then he showed me the river of the water of life, bright as crystal, flowing from the throne of God and of the Lamb, through the middle of the street of the city" (Rev. 22:1).

This water is available to all who want it. "And let him who is thirsty come, let him who desires take the water of life without price" (Rev. 22:17).

These scriptures present the Heart of Jesus as the source of the miraculous waters that well up to eternal life. We find this imagery revealed first to those who live in the desert in Israel and then to the whole human race. Those who find themselves thirsting in a spiritual desert are invited to drink freely of the life-giving waters and immerse themselves in the oasis of the Holy Spirit. These purifying waters both cleanse and refresh believers, helping them to become as pure as a new rain. In this state of purity, they become worthy to stand before the Father's throne and witness the creation of the New Jerusalem where God and His people will be forever inseparable.

Another scriptural passage that has played an important role in the development of the devotion to the Sacred Heart occurs in John's account of the Last Supper. Jesus said that one of His followers would betray Him, and John rested his head on Jesus. "One of his disciples, whom Jesus loved, was lying close to the breast of Jesus; so Simon Peter beckoned to him and said, 'Tell us who it is of whom he speaks.' So lying thus, close to the breast of Jesus, he said to him, 'Lord, who is it?'" (John 13:23–25).

This incident is so significant that it is mentioned again at the end of the Gospels. "Peter turned and saw following them the disciple whom Jesus loved, who had lain close to his breast at the supper and had said, 'Lord, who is it that is going to betray you?'" (John 21:20).

The early Christians attached a great deal of significance to this scene where John reclined in such a way that his head was directly above the Heart of Jesus, believing that this must have been a wonderful experience for him. Centuries later Saint Gertrude confirmed that this was so (see chapter 2).

John experienced a deep rapture when he rested his head near the Heart of Jesus. The following day he saw an instrument of destruction plunged into that Heart.

> So the soldiers came and broke the legs of the first, and of the other who had been crucified with him; but when they came to Jesus and saw that he was already dead, they did not break his legs. But one of the soldiers pierced his side with a spear, and at once there came out blood and water. He who saw it has borne witness—his testimony is true, and he knows that he tells the truth—that you may believe. For these things took place that the scripture might be fulfilled, 'Not a bone of him shall be broken.' And again another scripture says, 'They shall look on him whom they have pierced.' (John 19:32–37)

And so it was that a soldier pierced the Heart of Jesus. Saint John had received an outpouring of graces from that Heart the previous evening. He is the only one of the four evangelists who mentions the thrust of the spear. He attaches so much significance to it that he then immediately affirms it is true. John knew this incident was of the greatest importance, because it fulfilled several Old Testament prophecies. The first of these is from Exodus, where God gave instructions about how to prepare the Passover lamb. "You shall not break a bone of it" (Exod. 12:46).

Jesus is the New Covenant's Passover Lamb, the Lamb of God Who takes away the sins of the world. The other scripture Saint John referred to in his passage about the piercing of the Heart of Jesus was the mysterious prophecy from Zechariah that described people gazing on the one they had pierced in the context of a shower of blessings. "And I will pour out on the house of David and the inhabitants of Jerusalem a spirit of compassion and supplication, so that, when they look on him whom they have pierced, they shall mourn for him, as one mourns for an only child, and weep bitterly over him, as one weeps over a first-born" (Zech. 12:10).

And on the day the inhabitants of Jerusalem would behold the pierced Savior, a fountain of grace would spring forth. "On that day there shall be a fountain opened for the house of David and the inhabitants of Jerusalem to cleanse them from sin and uncleanness" (Zech. 13:1).

Another passage in Matthew related to the Sacred Heart devotion describes how an awesome and mysterious event accompanied the death of Jesus. "And behold, the curtain of the temple was torn in two, from top to bottom" (Matt. 27:51).

While the accounts in the Gospels are not specific, many biblical scholars have surmised that this is a reference to the veil in the temple that covered the Holy of Holies. The only person who could enter this inner sanctuary was the high priest, and he could enter only once a year on the day set aside for the expiation of sins, the Day of Atonement (Yom Kippur).

One of Saint Margaret Mary's letters suggests that it was indeed the veil of the Holy of Holies that was torn apart that day as the Heart of Jesus, which had also been torn, became the New Covenant's Holy of Holies. "He has given me to understand that His Sacred Heart is the Holy of Holies, the very sanctuary of love. He wishes that It be now recognized as the Mediator between God and men. He is all-powerful to bring them peace, turning aside the just punishments our sins have drawn upon us and obtaining mercy for us."

The letter to the Hebrews suggests the same idea. The following passage appears after the exposition of Psalm 40 (discussed above): "Therefore, brethren, since we have confidence to enter the sanctuary by the blood of Jesus, by the new and living way which he opened for us through the curtain, that is, through his flesh, and since we have a great priest over the house of God, let us draw near with a true heart in full assurance of faith, with our hearts sprinkled clean from an evil conscience and our bodies washed with pure water" (Heb. 10:19–22).

The last scriptural passage we will consider here concerns an invitation Jesus extended to Saint Thomas, which took place after the resurrection. "Then he said to Thomas, 'Put your finger here, and see my hands; and put out your hand, and place it in my side; do not be faithless, but believing.' Thomas answered him, 'My Lord and my God!'" (John 20:27–28).

Thomas became a believer, proclaiming Jesus as Lord, after Jesus gave him an invitation to enter the wound in His side leading to the Sacred Heart. Thomas had witnessed many miracles as he followed Jesus over the years, but his faith was confirmed when he approached the Heart that had triumphed over sin and death. Similarly, many Catholics have witnessed hundreds of miracles in their lives as the Son of God has miraculously appeared on their altars at the moment of consecration during Mass. Jesus invites all of us to overcome any doubts we may have, any frailty of faith, by entering the wound in His side and casting ourselves into His Sacred Heart. In that Heart, the inner sanctuary of love, the Holy of Holies, we can obtain unshakable faith and everlasting life as we learn to accept Jesus as our Lord and our God.

Eleven

The Promises of the Sacred Heart

And the Word became flesh and dwelt among us, full of grace and truth; we have beheld his glory, glory as of the only Son from the Father.

John 1:14

Truly, truly, I say to you, he who hears my word and believes him who sent me, has eternal life; he does not come into judgment, but has passed from death to life.

John 5:24

He is able for all time to save those who draw near to God through him, since he always lives to make intercession for them.

Hebrews 7:25

Jesus told Saint Margaret Mary that those who practice the devotion to His Sacred Heart would receive a torrent of graces so powerful that their effects will last throughout eternity. These blessings begin in this life by helping us to give up sin and become pure in the sight of the Father. The Holy Spirit guides us, leading us into the Heart of Christ.

Many people are familiar with a list of twelve promises that often appears in pamphlets and books about the Sacred Heart. The list usually appears as follows:

1. I will give them all the graces necessary in their state of life.
2. I will establish peace in their homes.
3. I will comfort them in all their afflictions.
4. I will be their secure refuge during life, and above all, in death.
5. I will bestow abundant blessings upon all their undertakings.
6. Sinners will find in My Heart the source and infinite ocean of mercy.
7. Lukewarm souls shall become fervent.
8. Fervent souls shall quickly mount to high perfection.

9. I will bless every place in which an image of My Heart is exposed and honored.
10. I will give to priests the gift of touching the most hardened hearts.
11. Those who promote this devotion shall have their names written in My Heart.
12. I promise you in the excessive mercy of My Heart that My all-powerful love will grant to those who receive Holy Communion on the First Fridays in nine consecutive months the grace of final perseverance; they shall not die in My disgrace, nor without receiving their sacraments. My divine Heart shall be their safe refuge in this last moment.

These twelve promises appear in the works of Saint Margaret Mary. However, they do not appear in the form of a list in her writings or in precisely the same words. Also, the list is not comprehensive, but it is a brief selection of the blessings related to the devotion. Many similar promises appear in the Bible. Below are excerpts from the letters of Saint Margaret Mary that illuminate the magnificent graces Jesus gives to disciples of His Heart. Many passages from scripture touch on the same topics.

Blessings for Sinners

"He has given me to understand that His Sacred Heart is the Holy of Holies, the very sanctuary of love. He wishes that It be now recognized as the Mediator between God and men. He is all powerful to bring them peace, turning aside the just punishments our sins have drawn upon us and obtaining mercy for us."

"For this is a last effort of the Savior to draw sinners to repentance and to give them abundantly efficacious and sanctifying graces to work out their salvation. By this means many will be saved from eternal damnation. Woe to those who do not want to profit by it! Let us constantly pray that His reign be established in all hearts. Let us contribute to that as much as we can. Let us spare neither our goods nor our energies."

"It seems to me that it is in this way He wishes to save many souls from eternal damnation, for this divine Heart is a fortress and a sure refuge for those fleeing from divine justice. God's wrath would otherwise overwhelm sinners in their sins because of the great number they are now committing. These stir up the divine anger of this Sacred Heart. It is an abyss of every kind of blessing. There we must lose ourselves so as to relish no longer the things of earth."

"Let us love this Sacred Heart which will be the altar on which we offer our sacrifices. Oh, how powerful is this Heart to appease the wrath of God aroused against us by our many sins! They have drawn down upon us all these calamities that afflict us. We must pray lest still worse things befall us. Prayer in common has great power with this Sacred Heart, which will turn aside the rigors of divine justice and place Itself between God's wrath and sinners and obtain mercy for them."

"It seems to me that Our Lord greatly desires His Sacred Heart to be honored in some special way, so that the effects of the Redemption may be renewed in souls. He wishes to make this Sacred Heart, as it were, a second Mediator between God and men, whose sins have so multiplied that it takes all His power to obtain mercy and the graces of salvation and sanctification which He longs to impart abundantly to them."

"As for your entering into His Sacred Heart: enter in! What should you fear, since He invites you to come in and rest there? Is It not the throne of mercy, where the most miserable are the most graciously received, provided love presents them in the abyss of their misery? And if we are tepid, cold, sinful, and imperfect, is It not a burning furnace in which we must be perfected and purified like gold in the crucible, so that we may become living victims completely immolated and sacrificed to His adorable designs? Do not be afraid, then, to abandon yourself without reserve to His loving providence. A child cannot perish in the arms of an omnipotent Father."

"When we commit some fault, we must hasten to this divine Heart to have Him put us back in the good graces of God the Father. To Him we must offer one of the virtues opposed to our fault, as His humility for our pride, and so on. By doing this lovingly, we will satisfy our debt to the divine justice as He has promised."

"With regard to your being afraid, I think our Lord will be pleased with you if you go to Him with the dispositions of the prodigal son, not letting fear destroy your confidence. It is not said, however, that this boy, once returned to his father, left him a second time!"

***

"Bring quickly the best robe, and put it on him; and put a ring on his hand, and shoes on his feet; and bring the fatted calf and kill it, and let us eat and make merry; for this my son was dead, and is alive again; he was lost, and is found" (Luke 15:22–24).

"If you turn to him with all your heart and with all your soul, to do what is true before him, then he will turn to you and will not hide his face from you" (Tob. 13:6).

"Behold, the days are coming, says the Lord, when I will make a new covenant with the house of Israel and the house of Judah, not like the covenant which I made with their fathers when I took them by the hand to bring them out of the land of Egypt, my covenant which they broke, though I was their husband, says the Lord. But this is the covenant which I will make with the house of Israel after those days, say the Lord: I will put my law within them, and I will write it upon their hearts; and I will be their God, and they shall be my people. And no longer shall each man teach his neighbor and each his brother, saying, 'Know the Lord,' for they shall all know me, from the least of them to the greatest, says the Lord; for I will forgive their iniquity, and I will remember their sin no more" (Jer. 31:33–34).

"I will heal their faithlessness, I will love them freely, for my anger has turned from them" (Hosea 14:4).

"On that day there shall be a fountain opened for the house of David and the inhabitants of Jerusalem to cleanse them from sin and unclean-ness" (Zech. 13:1).

"For I came not to call the righteous, but sinners" (Matt. 9:13).

"For God sent the Son into the world, not to condemn the world, but that the world might be saved through him" (John 3:17).

"While we were yet helpless, at the right time Christ died for the ungodly. Why, one will hardly die for a righteous man—though perhaps for a good man one will dare even to die. But God shows his love for us in that while we were yet sinners Christ died for us. Since, therefore, we are now justified by his blood, much more shall we be saved by him from the wrath of God. For if while we were enemies we were reconciled to God by the death of his Son, much more, now that we are reconciled, shall we be saved by his life" (Rom. 5:6–10).

"For God has not destined us for wrath, but to obtain salvation through our Lord Jesus Christ" (1 Thess. 5:9).

"Since therefore the children share in flesh and blood, he himself likewise partook of the same nature, that through death he might destroy him who has the power of death, that is, the devil, and deliver all those who through fear of death were subject to lifelong bondage. For surely it is not with angels that he is concerned but with the descendants of Abraham. Therefore he had to be made like his brethren in every respect, so that he might become a merciful and faithful high priest in the service of God, to make expiation for the sins of the people. For because he himself has suffered and been tempted, he is able to help those who are tempted" (Heb. 2:14–17).

***

The blessings for sinners give the grace of true repentance. They also give us a desire to make reparation for our own sins and those of others. A growing aversion to sin is one of the fruits of the devotion.

Blessings on Those Who Seek Spiritual Perfection

"This Sacred Heart contains an inexhaustible treasure of blessings and graces. I doubt whether there is any exercise of piety in the spiritual life as well adapted to raise a soul to the highest perfection in a short time and to make it taste the true sweetness one finds in the service of Jesus Christ. Yes, I am certain that if people knew how pleasing this devotion is to Jesus Christ, there would not be a Christian with so little love for this lovable Savior as not to practice it at once."

"This divine Heart is an inexhaustible fountain from which three streams are continually flowing. The first is the stream of mercy, which flows down upon sinners and brings the spirit of sorrow and repentance. The second is the stream of charity which brings relief to all those who are suffering under some need, and especially those who are striving for perfection. These will find, through the help of the holy angels, the means of overcoming their difficulties. The third is the stream of love and light for perfect friends whom He wills to unite with Himself. To these He will communicate His knowledge and way of life, in order that they may give themselves up completely to furthering His glory, each one in his own way. The Blessed Virgin will be a special patron of these. She will bring them to a perfect life. Moreover, this divine Heart will be a sure refuge and a harbor of safety at the hour of death for all those who have honored It during life. It will protect and defend them."

In one letter Saint Margaret Mary addressed her brother, who was a parish priest. "You have no idea how much pleasure you give me by being so zealous for the glory of the Sacred Heart of our divine Savior. That way lies, I think, one of the shortest roads to our sanctification. I am as eager for yours as for my own, you may be sure. But, dear brother, we must do ourselves violence if we are to arrive at the perfection God asks of us. That is no small degree of perfection, for He wishes to make a saint of you. Yes, He wishes to make a saint of you if only you are willing to cooperate with His plans and follow the lights He gives you. I am confident He will not refuse you the graces necessary for that."

"Let us love Him, then, Who is the only love of our souls, because He first has loved us and still does love us with such a constant and burning love in the Blessed Sacrament. We have but to love this Saint of saints in order to become saints. Who, indeed, shall stop us from becoming saints, as long as we have hearts with which to love and bodies with which to suffer! Yet can one, alas, suffer when one loves? No, dear friend, there is no more suffering for those who ardently love the Sacred Heart of our lovable Jesus. Sorrow, humiliation, contempt, contradiction, everything most bitter to nature is changed into love in this adorable Heart, which wishes to be loved most purely. He wishes to have all without reserve, He wishes to do everything in us without any resistance on our part. Let us surrender, then, to His power, let us entrust ourselves to Him and let Him act. Then we shall see that He will without fail employ all the means necessary for our perfection. That work will soon be finished if only we place no obstacles in the way. For frequently, by wanting to do too much ourselves, we force Him to allow us to act alone, and to withdraw from us in displeasure. Ah, how careful is one who loves Him perfectly not to resist Him!"

"I cannot help but believe that if Our Lord makes you persevere in the good desires He gives you of loving and honoring His Sacred Heart, you will have a special place in it. He will take care to perfect you in proportion as you show your love for Him by practicing its virtues."

"It should be enough for you that you have given yourself into His care. In so far as you forget yourself He will take special care to make you perfect, purify you, sanctify you."

"As long as He is satisfied, that is enough. Leave Him free to act as He wishes. Let your occupation be to love Him. You should be careful not to resist Him nor place any obstacles in the way of His designs. You will find that He will cause you to make great progress in a short time without your perceiving it."

***

"With weeping they shall come, and with consolations I will lead them back, I will make them walk by brooks of water, in a straight path in which they shall not stumble" (Jer. 31:9).

"You, therefore, must be perfect, as your heavenly father is perfect" (Matt. 5:48).

"Beloved, let us love one another; for love is of God, and he who loves is born of God and knows God. He who does not love does not know God; for God is love. In this the love of God was made manifest among us, that God sent his only Son into the world, so that we might live through him. In this is love, not that we loved God but that he loved us and sent his Son to be the expiation for our sins. Beloved, if God so loved us, we also ought to love one another. No man has ever seen God; if we love one another, God abides in us and his love is perfected in us" (1 John 4:7–12).

***

The Sacred Heart calls sinners to repentance, but He doesn't stop there. This devotion gives ordinary people the means to make extraordinary progress on the path of spiritual perfection.

Blessings on Laypeople

"The laity will find in this lovable devotion all the helps necessary for their state in life: peace in their families, consolation in their work, the blessing of heaven on all their undertakings, consolation in their afflictions. It is especially in this Sacred Heart that they will find a refuge during their whole life and principally at the hour of death. O, how sweet it is to die after having practiced a tender and constant devotion to the Sacred Heart of Jesus Christ!"

"It is perfectly clear that there is no one in the world who would not receive every kind of help from heaven if he had a truly grateful love for Jesus Christ. It is such a love one shows by practicing devotion to His Sacred Heart."

***

"They brought him all the sick, those afflicted with various diseases and pains, demoniacs, epileptics, and paralytics, and he healed them" (Matt. 4:24).

"If you ask anything in my name, I will do it" (John 14:14).

"And this is the confidence which we have in him, that if we ask anything according to his will, he hears us. And if we know that he hears us in whatever we ask, we know that we have obtained the requests made of him" (1 John 5:14–15).

***

The Sacred Heart gives His love in such profusion that it affects entire families. Many receive temporal blessings as well as a rich spiritual life. However, God doesn't grant temporal blessings that would interfere with His goal of guiding us to eternal life.

Blessings for Vowed Religious Who Practice the Devotion

"Strive especially to get religious to embrace it, for they will draw so much help from it that they will need no other means to bring them back to their first fervor. It will restore the most exact observance in the most lax communities and bring to the height of perfection those who live a truly observant life."

***

"If a man loves me, he will keep my word, and my Father will love him, and we will come to him and make our home with him" (John 14:23).

"Now the company of those who believed were of one heart and soul, and no one said that any of the things which he possessed was his own, but they had everything in common. And with great power the Apostles gave their testimony to the resurrection of the Lord

Jesus, and great grace was upon them all"
(Acts 4:32–33).

"He who is united to the Lord becomes one
spirit with him" (1 Cor. 6:17).

Blessings Related to the Consecration
to the Sacred Heart

"If you only knew how much merit and glory
there is in honoring this loving Heart of the adorable Jesus and how great will be the recompense
for those who, having consecrated themselves to
It, strive only to honor It! Yes, it seems to me that
this intention alone will gain for them more merit,
will make their actions more pleasing before
God, than everything else they can do without
this intention."

"When we are completely consecrated and
pledged to this adorable Heart, to love and honor
It as much as we can, abandoning ourselves
entirely to It, Our Lord takes care of us and sees
to it that, is spite of all storms, we come safely
into the harbor of salvation."

"I tell you plainly that I think you will do a
thing very pleasing to God if you consecrate
and offer yourself to this Sacred Heart, if you
have not already done so. You must receive Holy
Communion on some first Friday of the month

and, after it, offer Him the sacrifice of yourself by dedicating to Him your whole being to be employed in His service and to procure for Him all the glory, love, and praise you can."

"I assure you that I am convinced that persons consecrated to this Sacred Heart will never perish. Neither will they fall under Satan's dominion by mortal sin if, after having given themselves completely to the Sacred Heart, they strive to honor, love, and glorify Him as much as they can, by conforming themselves to His holy maxims in everything."

"I am convinced there is no shorter way to perfection, no surer way to salvation, than to be consecrated to this divine Heart and to render It all the homage of love, honor, and praise of which we are capable."

"The devil is very afraid of seeing this good work accomplished because of the glory it will give the Sacred Heart of Our Lord Jesus Christ. For the souls of the many who consecrate themselves completely to Him, and love, honor, and glorify Him, will be saved by their devotion to this loving Heart."

"I am as though in a bottomless abyss, where He shows me treasures of love and grace for those who consecrate themselves to Him and work unstintingly to render Him and procure for Him all the honor, love, and glory they can."

"He intends to restore life to many by this means by withdrawing many from the road to perdition and destroying the empire of Satan in souls, in order to establish the empire of His love. He will not allow any to perish who are consecrated to Him, and who give Him all their homage and love with a sincere good will, and get others to do the same in so far as they can."

In one letter Saint Margaret Mary wrote that Jesus longs for love.

"He shows how great is this longing of His by promising that all those who consecrate themselves to Him and are devoted to Him in order to give Him this pleasure, who do all in their power to give Him and cause others to give Him all the love, honor, and glory they can by the means He provides, will never be lost. He will be their secure refuge against all the snares of their enemies. Especially at the hour of death this divine Heart will receive them lovingly and make their salvation sure. He will take care to sanctify them and make them great before His heavenly Father in proportion as they work earnestly to extend the reign of His love in the hearts of men."

In another letter Saint Margaret Mary described devotion to the Sacred Heart "as one of the last efforts of His love to save men. He showed this clearly in a special vision showing His divine Heart pierced with love for men.

He will make their salvation sure, He will not allow anyone consecrated to Him to be lost. He has a great desire to be known, loved and honored by His creatures. In this way He can satisfy to some extent the ardent desire to spread His love. He will shower graces upon them for their salvation and sanctification. He will be their sure refuge at the hour of death. He will take them under His protection and defend them from their enemies. To obtain all this, of course, they must lead lives in conformity with His divine maxims."

***

"I do not pray that thou shouldst take them out of the world, but that thou shouldst keep them from the evil one. They are not of the world, even as I am not of the world. Sanctify them in the truth; thy word is truth. As thou didst send me into the world, so I have sent them into the world. And for their sake I consecrate myself, that they also may be consecrated in truth" (John 17:15–19).

"I have been crucified with Christ; it is no longer I who live, but Christ who lives in me; and the life I now live in the flesh I live by faith in the Son of God, who loved me and gave himself for me" (Gal. 2:20).

"Therefore be imitators of God, as beloved children. And walk in love, as Christ loved us and gave himself up for us, a fragrant offering and sacrifice to God" (Eph. 5:1–2).

"For it was fitting that he, for whom and by whom all things exist, in bringing many sons to glory, should make the pioneer of their salvation perfect through suffering. For he who sanctifies and those who are sanctified have all one origin" (Heb. 2:10–11).

***

A personal act of consecration to the Sacred Heart is a critical part of the devotion. Everyone who practices the devotion may make such an act after prayerful consideration. The act of consecration can employ one's own words or the prayer of consecration written by Saint Margaret Mary. The text of the prayer is included in a letter she wrote to Sister Felice-Madeleine de la Barge:

I, N.N., give and consecrate to the Sacred Heart of Our Lord Jesus Christ my person and my life, my actions, trials and sufferings, so that I may no longer wish to make use of any part of my being except to honor, love, and glorify Him. This is my irrevocable will, to belong entirely to Him and to do everything for His love, and I renounce with all my heart anything that can be displeasing to Him. I take Thee, then, O Sacred Heart, as my salvation, the remedy of my infirmities, the reparation for all the sins of my life and my sure refuge at the hour of my death. Be, then, O Heart of Goodness, my justification with God the Father, and turn aside the blows of His just wrath. O Heart of Love, I place all my confidence in Thee. I fear everything from my malice but hope everything from Thy goodness. Consume in me everything that can displease or resist Thee. May Thy pure love impress Thee so deeply in my heart that I can never forget Thee, nor ever be separated from Thee. I conjure Thee by Thy boundless goodness to write my name in They Sacred Heart, for I wish to live and die as Thy slave. Amen.

Blessings Related to Religious Fervor

"You have never seen such fervor as this devotion is enkindling in hearts. May God be blessed eternally!"

"I must tell you how consoled I am by the fervor shown by people here. Many make novenas and forthwith their requests are granted."

"The devotion produces rich fruit and makes a great change in those who are devoted to it and earnestly practice it."

***

"Go and tell John what you have seen and heard: the blind receive their sight, the lame walk, lepers are cleansed, and the deaf hear, the dead are raised up, the poor have good news preached to them" (Luke 7:22).

"And from his fullness we have all received, grace upon grace" (John 1:16).

"The hour is coming, and now is, when the true worshipers will worship the Father in spirit and truth, for such the Father seeks to worship him. God is Spirit, and those who worship him must worship in Spirit and truth" (John 4:23–24).

***

The Sacred Heart transforms souls who come to Him. Those who practice the devotion find themselves in an intimate relationship with the Blessed Trinity. Their faith grows as they gain more confidence in God, asking Him for ever greater blessings. Because they have received such blessings, their faith grows even more. The devotion produces a dazzling spiral of confidence in Jesus that leads to heaven.

Blessings on Those Who Work for the Salvation of Others

"My divine Master has made known to me that those who labor for the salvation of souls will work with the greatest success and know how to touch the most hardened hearts if they have a tender devotion to His Sacred Heart, and strive to instill it in others and to establish it everywhere."

"There is nothing sweeter or more gentle and at the same time stronger or more efficacious than the unction of the ardent charity of this lovable Heart. To convert the most hardened sinners and penetrate the coldest hearts He will make the word of His preachers and of His faithful friends like a flaming sword. It will melt by His love the coldest hearts."

***

"Follow me, and I will make you fishers of men" (Matt. 4:19).

***

This ability to melt hardened hearts is one of the most spectacular fruits of the devotion. One famous example is the life of Saint Catherine of Siena. Saint Catherine once had a mystical experience in which Jesus invited her to drink from the wound in His side. After this experience she gained a reputation for touching the hearts of sinners through her fervent prayers. At times, she didn't even meet the people she prayed for. Yet they received graces of repentance that changed their lives and led to their salvation.

Saint Gertrude also had this gift. During her lifetime she gained such a reputation for holiness that many people sought her advice. A member of her community described the effect Saint Gertrude would have on people.

"Many testified to having been more profoundly moved by a single word of hers than by a long sermon by any of the best preachers. This is attested by the tears of sincere contrition shed by those who came to speak to her. Sometimes they came with rebellious hearts, seemingly indomitable, but after hearing only a few words from her they were so moved by compunction that they promised to yield in everything and to do whatever was their duty."

Blessings Granted to Those Who Promote the Devotion

"Eventually this divine Heart shall reign in spite of all those who oppose Him. Satan and all his followers will be confounded. Fortunate shall they be whom He uses to establish His empire! It seems to me He is like a king who does not think of giving rewards while he is making his conquests and overcoming his enemies, but only then indeed when he has come to reign victoriously on his throne. The adorable Heart of Jesus wishes to establish His reign of love in the hearts of all, to destroy and bring to ruin the kingdom of Satan. It seems to me He has so great a desire of doing this that He promises great rewards to men of good will who work for it with all their heart according to the strength and lights He gives them...But this is the kind of devotion that cannot be forced or imposed on anyone. It is enough to make it known and then leave to this divine Heart the work of entering the souls He has prepared by His grace. Fortunate indeed are these!"

"I want to pour forth acts of thanksgiving and acknowledgement to the goodness of this divine Heart for the great favors He has given us, for having deigned to use us to make Him known, loved and honored. He has promised infinite blessings to those who, under His inspiration, work with all their might for this end."

"Everything must be done gently and tactfully, with the means He furnishes you. Leave to Him the success of everything, without desiring or wishing more. He will give you to understand in each instance what He wants you to do. This, it seems to me, is your means of sanctification. For in proportion as you work at this, this divine Heart will sanctify you with His very own holiness."

"He will reward you out of His infinite treasures. So I trust that you will lose nothing and that He Himself will be your reward."

"O, if only I could, and if only it were permitted me to reveal what He has given me to know of the reward those who labor to make Him known and loved will receive from this adorable Heart, you would agree with me as to how fortunate are those He makes use of to carry out His designs!"

"He has not allowed me to speak of the reward He promises those He makes use of to carry out this holy work in order that they may labor disinterestedly for His glory, having in view only His pure love."

"The divine Heart will reward not only you personally but your relatives as well. He looks upon them with an eye of mercy and will help them in all their needs provided only they approach Him in confidence. He will remember forever all they do for His glory."

"Your name will be written indelibly in this Sacred Heart."

"You ought to consider yourself fortunate at being employed in this holy work. Do not be afraid to forget self for its sake. Complete absence of self-interest is the true disposition required in those who promote this devotion.

"He will not forget you in your work. He looks upon you with pleasure and applies Himself to the task of purifying and sanctifying you in order to unite you perfectly with Himself while you are working for His glory. He loves you, and you must do all in your power to make Him some return."

***

"Those who honor me I will honor" (1 Sam. 2:30).

"So everyone who acknowledges me before men, I also will acknowledge before my Father who is in heaven" (Matt. 10:32).

***

Saint Margaret Mary states that an infinite reward awaits those who promote this devotion. God didn't allow her to reveal the details. Some souls may spend their entire lives promoting the devotion. Others contribute in small but significant ways. Giving someone a ride to church on first Fridays can help. Many Catholic bookstores carry pamphlets designed to introduce people to the Sacred Heart; an easy way to promote the devotion is to buy a few of these and leave them in the vestibule of a church. Those who are homebound can contribute by praying for the spread of the devotion.

Blessings for Families Who Honor the Image of the Sacred Heart

"Since He is the source of all blessings, He will shower them on every place where an image of this Sacred Heart shall be honored, because His love urges Him to dispense the inexhaustible treasures of His sanctifying and salutary graces to all souls of good will. He is looking for empty hearts devoid of self-love to fill with the sweet unction of His ardent charity, to consume and transform completely into Himself. He is seeking humble and submissive souls that want nothing but the accomplishment of His good pleasure. Moreover, by this means He will restore broken families and protect those that are in any difficulty."

***

"Seek first his kingdom and his righteousness, and all these things shall be yours as well" (Matt. 6:33).

"Let the children come to me, and do not hinder them; for to such belongs the kingdom of God" (Luke 18:16).

"For this reason I bow my knees before the Father, from whom every family in heaven and on earth is named, that according to the riches of his glory he may grant you to be strengthened with might through his Spirit in the inner man, and that Christ may dwell in your hearts through faith; that you, being rooted and grounded in love, may have power to comprehend with all the saints what is the breadth and length and height and depth, and to know the love of Christ which surpasses knowledge, that you may be filled with all the fullness of God" (Eph. 3:14–19).

"Behold, I stand at the door and knock; if anyone hears my voice and opens the door, I will come in to him and eat with him, and he with me" (Rev. 3:20).

***

Those who practice the devotion will want to have a picture or statue of the Sacred Heart in their homes. The image is a source of inspiration and a reminder of the Lordship of Jesus. One way to honor the image of the Sacred Heart in the home is through a formal enthronement ceremony. Father Francis Larkin's book, *Enthronement of the Sacred Heart*, is an excellent guide that offers various enthronement ceremonies.

For Communities That Honor the Image of the Sacred Heart

"He will spread the soothing unction of His ardent charity on every religious community in which this divine image is honored. He will turn aside the blows of the just wrath of God by restoring them to His grace when through sin they have fallen from it."

***

"I do not pray for these only, but also for those who believe in me through their word, that they may all be one; even as thou, Father, art in me, and I in thee, that they also may be in us, so that the world may believe that thou has sent me. The glory which thou hast given me I have given to them, that they may be one even as we are one, I in them and thou in me, that they may become perfectly one, so that the world may know that thou has sent me and hast loved them even as thou hast loved me" (John 17:20–23).

"He who did not spare his own Son but gave him up for us all, will he not also give us all things with him?" (Rom. 8:32).

"Be filled with the Spirit, addressing one another in psalms and hymns and spiritual songs, singing and making melody to the Lord with all your heart, always and for everything giving thanks in the name of our Lord Jesus Christ to God the Father" (Eph. 5:18–20).

"And let the peace of Christ rule in your hearts, to which indeed you were called in the one body. And be thankful" (Col. 3:15).

The Great Promise

Saint Margaret Mary recounted the following words Jesus spoke to her on a Friday during Holy Communion: "I promise you, in the excessive mercy of My Heart, that Its all-powerful love will grant all those who communicate on nine consecutive first Fridays of the month the grace of final repentance. They will not die in My disfavor nor without receiving their sacraments. My divine Heart shall be their secure refuge in their last moments."

***

"I am the bread of life; he who comes to me shall not hunger, and he who believes in me shall never thirst" (John 6:35).

"Death is swallowed up in victory. O death, where is thy victory? O death, where is thy sting?" (1 Cor. 15:54–55).

"Behold, the dwelling of God is with men. He shall dwell with them, and they shall be his people, and God himself will be with them; he will wipe away every tear from their eyes, and death shall be no more, neither shall there be mourning nor crying nor pain any more, for the former things have passed away" (Rev. 21:3–4).

***

Here we have a promise of eternal life for all those who honor the Sacred Heart by receiving the Bread of Life. Jesus intends this not as an automatic blessing that can be abused by returning to practices that displease Him but as a way of bringing us closer to Him. This blessing is granted to those who practice devotion to the Sacred Heart by making a sincere effort to turn away from sin and abandon themselves to God's holy will. It involves a long-term commitment in that the Eucharist must be received on nine first Fridays, and they must be consecutive. Many people, despite their efforts, will find that they are unable to keep this commitment the first time they try. Some set of circumstances will arise, preventing them from receiving Communion on one of the first Fridays, and they will have to start again.

This setback should be viewed as a blessing, because it often increases our fervor and determination to enter the Heart of Jesus. Reception of Communion on first Fridays should be done in honor of the Passion and the Sacred Heart of Jesus, which was pierced for love of us on Calvary. In addition, this practice is designed to inculcate the habit of honoring the Heart of Jesus in the Eucharist through the frequent reception of Communion and by making visits to the Blessed Sacrament.

Bibliography

Allegra, Gabriel. *Mary's Immaculate Heart: A Way to God*. Translated by Joachim Daleiden. Chicago: Franciscan Herald Press, 1985.

De Liguori, Alphonsus. *The Holy Eucharist*. Brooklyn, NY: Redemptorist Fathers, 1934.

Arnoudt, Peter J. *The Imitation of the Sacred Heart of Jesus*. Rockford, IL: Tan Books and Publishers, 1974.

Baldwin, Anne B. *Catherine of Siena: A Biography*. Huntington, IN: Our Sunday Visitor, 1987.

Barbet, Pierre. *A Doctor at Calvary*. Garden City, NY: Image Books, 1963.

Bovenmars, Jan G. *A Biblical Spirituality of the Heart*. Staten Island, NY: Alba House, 1991.

Van den Broek, Silvere, ed. *The Spiritual Legacy of Sister Mary of the Holy Trinity*. Rockford, IL: Tan Books and Publishers, 1981.

Bougaud, Emile. *The Life of St. Margaret Mary Alacoque*. Rockford, IL: Tan Books and Publishers, 2002.

Catherine of Siena. *The Dialogue*. Translated by Suzanne Noffke. Mahwah, NJ: Paulist Press, 1980.

Charmot, Francois. *The Sacred Heart and Modern Life*. Translated by Kathryn Sullivan. New York: P. J. Kenedy & Sons, 1952.

Crawley-Boevey, Mateo. *Jesus, King of Love*. Boston: Daughters of St. Paul, 1978.

Crawley-Boevey, Mateo. *Twenty Holy Hours*. Boston: Daughters of St. Paul, 1978.

Cristiani, Leon. *Saint Margaret Mary Alacoque and the Promises of the Sacred Heart*. Translated by M. Angeline Bouchard. Boston: Daughters of St. Paul, 1975.

Croiset, John. *The Devotion to the Sacred Heart of Jesus*. Translated by Patrick O'Connell. Rockford, IL: Tan Books and Publishers, 1988.

Duboin, Alain-Marie. *The Life and Message of Sister Mary of the Holy Trinity*. Translated by Mary Douglas Chomeau. Rockford, IL: Tan Books and Publishers, 1987.

Kowalska, Faustina. *Divine Mercy in my Soul*. Stockbridge, MA: Marian Press, 1987.

Kowalska, Faustina. *The Letters of Saint Faustina*. Cracow: Misericordia Publications, 2005.

Fox, Robert J. *Immaculate Heart of Mary: True Devotion*. Huntington, IN: Our Sunday Visitor, 1986.

Sales, Francis de. *Introduction to the Devout Life*. Translated by John K. Ryan. Garden City, NY: Image Books, 1972.

Sales, Francis de, and Jane Frances de Chantal. *Letters of Spiritual Direction.* Translated by Peronne Marie Thibert. Mahwah, NJ: Paulist Press, 1988.

Sales, Francis de. *Treatise on the Love of God.* 2 vols. Translated by John K. Ryan. Rockford, IL: Tan Books and Publishers, 1975.

Galot, Jean. *The Eucharistic Heart.* Translated by Sister Aine Hayde. Dublin, Ireland: Veritas Publications, 1990.

Galot, Jean. *The Heart of Christ.* Translated by John Chapin. Westminster, MD: Newman Press, 1955.

Gertrude the Great. *The Herald of Divine Love.* Translated by Margaret Winkworth. Mahwah, NJ: Paulist Press, 1993.

Gertrude the Great. *The Life and Revelations of St. Gertrude.* Translated by a sister of the Convent of Poor Clares in Kenmare, Ireland. Westminster, MD: Christian Classics, 1975.

Gertrude the Great. *Spiritual Exercises.* Translated by Gertrud Jaron Lewis and Jack Lewis. Kalamazoo, MI: Cistercian Publications, 1989.

Gaitley, Michael E. *Consoling the Heart of Jesus.* Stockbridge, MA: Marian Press, 2010.

Gottemoller, Bartholomew, ed. *Words of Love.* Rockford, IL: Tan Books and Publishers, 1985.

Griffin, Michael D. *God, the Joy of My Life: Saint Teresa of the Andes.* Hubertus, WI: Teresian Charism Press, 1995.

Griffin, Michael D. *Testimonies to Saint Teresa of the Andes*. Washington, DC: Teresian Charism Press, 1995.

Haring, Bernard. *Heart of Jesus: Symbol of Redeeming Love*. Liguori, MO: Liguori Publications, 1983.

Chantal, Jane Frances de. *St. Wings to the Lord: Thoughts on Prayer*. Boston: Daughters of St. Paul, 1987.

Eudes, John. *The Sacred Heart of Jesus*. New York: P. J. Kenedy & Sons, 1946.

John Paul II. *Angelus Meditations on the Litany of the Sacred Heart of Jesus*. Huntington, IN: Our Sunday Visitor, 1992.

John Paul II. *Holy Father, Sacred Heart: The Wisdom of John Paul II on the Greatest Catholic Devotion*. Edited by Carl J. Moell. New York: Crossroad Publishing, 2004.

Konz, F. *The Sacred Heart of Christ*. New York: Benziger Brothers, 1936.

Kosicki, George W. *Revelations of Divine Mercy*. Ann Arbor, MI: Servant Publications, 1996.

Kubicki, James. *A Heart on Fire*. Notre Dame, IN: Ave Maria, 2012.

Claret de La Touche, Louise Margaret. *The Book of Infinite Love*. Translated by Patrick O'Connell. Rockford, IL: Tan Books and Publishers, 1979

Claret de La Touche, Louise Margaret. *The Sacred Heart and the Priesthood*. Translated by Patrick O'Connell. Rockford, IL: Tan Books and Publishers, 1979.

Larkin, Francis. *Enthronement of the Sacred Heart*. Boston: Daughters of St. Paul, 1978.

Larkin, Francis. *Understanding the Heart*. San Francisco: Ignatius Press, 1980.

LaVigne, Ruth H. *The Life of Saint Claude de la Colombiere*. Boston: Daughters of St. Paul, 1992.

Montfort, Louis Marie de. *True Devotion to the Blessed Virgin*. Bay Shore, NY: Montfort Publications, 1980.

Claret de la Touche, Louise Margaret. *The Book of Infinite Love*. Rockford, IL: Tan Books and Publishers, 1979.

Maloney, George A. *Entering into the Heart of Jesus: Meditations on the Indwelling Trinity in St. John's Gospel*. Staten Island, NY: Alba House, 1988.

Alacoque, Margaret Mary. *The Autobiography of Saint Margaret Mary*. Translated by the Sisters of the Visitation. Rockford, IL: Tan Books and Publishers, 1986.

Alacoque, Margaret Mary. *Jesus Reveals His Heart: Letters of Saint Margaret Mary Alacoque*. Translated by Clarence A. Herbst. Boston: Daughters of St. Paul, 1980.

Alacoque, Margaret Mary. *Thoughts and Sayings of Saint Margaret Mary*. Translated by the Sisters of the Visitation. Rockford, IL: Tan Books and Publishers, 1986.

Menendez, Josefa. *The Way of Divine Love*. Rockford, IL: Tan Books and Publishers, 1972.

Mechthild of Magdeburg. *The Flowing Light of the Godhead*. Translated by Frank Tobin. Mahwah, NJ: Paulist Press, 1998.

Michalenko, Sophia. *The Life of Faustina Kowalska*. Cincinnati: St. Anthony Messenger Press, 1999.

Most, William. *The Heart Has Its Reasons: The Sacred Heart of Jesus and the Immaculate Heart of Mary*. Libertyville, IL: Prow Books/Franciscan Marytown Press, 1985.

Myers, Rawley. *Jesus Is Here: Devotions to the Sacred Heart and Precious Blood*. Huntington, IN: Our Sunday Visitor Books, 1986.

Newman, John Henry Cardinal. *Taking on the Heart of Christ: Meditations and Devotions*. Denville, NJ: Dimension Books.

Odell, Catherine M. *Faustina: Apostle of Divine Mercy*. Huntington, IN: Our Sunday Visitor Books, 1998.

O'Donnell, Timothy T. *Heart of the Redeemer*. San Francisco: Ignatius Press, 1992.

Prevot, Andre. *Love, Peace and Joy: Devotion to the Sacred Heart of Jesus According to St. Gertrude*. Rockford, IL: Tan Books and Publishers, 1984.

Ratzinger, Joseph. *Behold the Pierced One*. Translated by Graham Harrison. San Francisco: Ignatius Press, 1986.

Rowe, Margaret. *God Is Love: Saint Teresa Margaret; Her Life*. Washington, DC: Institute of Carmelite Studies, 2003.

Saint-Jure, Jean Baptiste, and Claude de la Colombiere. *The Secret of Peace and Happiness.* Translated by Paul Garvin. Staten Island, NY: Alba House, 1961.

Siepak, M. Elzbieta. *A Gift from God for our Times: The Life and Mission of St. Faustina.* Cracow: Wydawnictwo Misericordia, 2007.

Smith, Herbert F. *Homilies on the Heart of Jesus and the Apostleship of Prayer.* Staten Island, NY: Alba House, 2000.

Teresa of the Andes. *Letters of Saint Teresa of the Andes.* Translated by Michael D. Griffin. Hubertus, WI: Teresian Charism Press, 1994.

Therese of Lisieux. *General Correspondence.* 2 vols. Translated by John Clarke. Washington, DC: Institute of Carmelite Studies, 1982.

Therese of Lisieux. *The Story of a Soul.* Translated by John Clarke. Washington, DC: Institute of Carmelite Studies, 1975, 1976, 1996.

Therese of Lisieux. *The Poetry of Saint Therese of Lisieux.* Translated by Donald Kinney, O.C.D. Washington, DC: Institute of Carmelite Studies, 1996.

Verheylezoon, Louis. *Devotion to the Sacred Heart.* Rockford, IL: Tan Books and Publishers, 1978.

Woodruff, Sue. *Meditations with Mechthild of Magdeburg.* Santa Fe, NM: Bear, 1982.

Additional Copyright Notices

About the Author

Philip Michael Bulman was born and raised in Philadelphia. He holds a master's degree in journalism from Northwestern University and is the author of several books, including *Replenish the Earth*, a novel of the early Christian church. Bulman currently divides his time between the United States and Asia.

Made in the USA
Lexington, KY
19 March 2015